FOLLOW ME!

by Charles Hunter

ISBN 0-917726-35-9

All scripture quotations are taken from the Living Bible, Tyndale House Publishers, except where otherwise designated.

KJV - King James Version
NIV - The New International Version
RSV - Revised Standard Version

For information about the City of Light Video teaching tapes, audio tapes, and price list of Hunter Books, write to:

HUNTER BOOKS
City of Light
201 McClellan Road
Kingwood, Texas 77339, U.S.A

In the event your Christian Bookstore does not have any of the books written by Charles and Frances Hunter or published by Hunter Books, please write for price list and order form from HUNTER BOOKS.

God and Jesus surely must have appraised all the rich treasures they own, selected the very best, and opened the windows of heaven to send my beloved Frances to me!

To the most Fabulous woman on earth, I dedicate this book—my own wife, my Frances!

Your
Charles

BOOKS
BY CHARLES♥FRANCES HUNTER

A CONFESSION A DAY KEEPS THE DEVIL AWAY
ANGELS ON ASSIGNMENT
ARE YOU TIRED?
BORN AGAIN! WHAT DO YOU MEAN?
COME ALIVE
DON'T LIMIT GOD
FOLLOW ME
GOD IS FABULOUS
GOD'S ANSWER TO FAT...LOOSE IT!
GOD'S CONDITIONS FOR PROSPERITY
HOT LINE TO HEAVEN
HOW TO MAKE YOUR MARRIAGE EXCITING
IF YOU REALLY LOVE ME...
IMPOSSIBLE MIRACLES
IN JESUS' NAME!
IT'S SO SIMPLE (formerly HANG LOOSE WITH JESUS)
LET'S GO WITNESSING (formerly GO, MAN, GO)
MEMORIZING MADE EASY
MY LOVE AFFAIR WITH CHARLES
NUGGETS OF TRUTH
POSSESSING THE MIND OF CHRIST
P.T.L.A. (Praise the Lord, Anyway!)
SIMPLE AS A.B.C.
SINCE JESUS PASSED BY
the fabulous SKINNIE MINNIE RECIPE BOOK
SUPERNATURAL HORIZONS (from Glory to Glory)
THE DEVIL WANTS YOUR MIND
THE TWO SIDES OF A COIN
THIS WAY UP!
TO HEAL THE SICK
WHY SHOULD "I" SPEAK IN TONGUES???

FOREWORD

"As he walked by the Sea of Galilee, he saw two brothers, Simon who is called Peter and Andrew his brother, casting a net into the sea; for they were fishermen. And he said to them, 'Follow me, and I will make you fishers of men.' "

Two thousand years later this same scene was reenacted with the same Jesus, the only difference was the man and the occupation.

Charles Hunter, Certified Public Accountant, church worker for many years, felt the drawing power of that same man who called Peter and Andrew from their nets. He called Charles Hunter from his accounting world with the same magnet he had used on the disciples and the same power fell on him that fell on them.

The twentieth century isn't any different than the first century, nor are the people involved. Nor is the way into complete discipleship any different now than it was then.

It all hinges on what we do when Jesus says "Follow Me!"

My heart thrilled the first time I met Charles Hunter to discover the call God had put on his life.

You, too, will thrill with every word and page as you discover how in these days and times, the same thing can happen in your life.

Frances Hunter
(Mrs. Charles Hunter)

TABLE OF CONTENTS

WHAT IS
OUR HERITAGE

Businessmen can have peace and prosperity!

Businessmen can have joy, happiness, freedom, and success simultaneously!

Businessmen can be free of pressures which bring on heart attacks and ulcers and frustrations and still be right in the middle of the activities that keep the business world turning!

Tough business and tender love do go together to bring about abundance!

Patience can come when deadlines are closing in on us. We can have sternness and gentleness in successfully negotiating business deals! When someone else's anger heats to a boiling point, we can have self control!

We can be kind to a competitor and still get our full share of the market!

We can be good to employees, associates, customers or clients, competitors—at all times and be a winner in the business world!

HOW!

First of all, we must WANT to! The enthusiastic teacher in high school who was faithfully giving a final thrust to shove us out of our secure nest into the vast world ahead said "Hitch your wagon to a star! Set your sights high! If you want to be a millionaire, think you will be, and don't be stopped with anything until you are one! Think positive! Go into deep water if you want to float a battleship or catch a big fish!" Drive! Drive! Drive!

This advice is good and has a lot to do with success, because success requires intelligence, hard work, positive thinking and perseverance. But total success is a balance during life, victory at the end of life on earth, and thereafter an eternal life of the highest order. The richest man on earth can be a total failure within himself and be a pauper in hell for eternity; yet that same rich man can have all the fruit of the Spirit within and have a whole year 'round orchard of fruit for eternity.

What is the road to total, balanced success? Jesus said "I am the way, the truth, and the life." That's not a verse of a poem—that's a fact we can stake our very life on—our personal life, our business life, our social life, our eternal life! It's a foundation which cannot be shaken or moved or changed. Jesus is the rock of our salvation. He is the foundation upon which all else is built.

And what does Jesus say:

"I have come to give you life and give it more abundantly!"

"Charles" (or Simon or Bill), "go out where it is deeper and let down your nets and you will catch a lot of fish!" (Luke 5:4)

"Bring all the tithes into the storehouse so that there will be food enough in my Temple; if you

2

do, I will open up the windows of heaven for you and pour out a blessing so great you won't have room enough to take it in! Try it! Let me prove it to you!" (Malachi 3:10)

Wow! What an offer made by God himself! It has much more potential and much more certainty than the inspirational theories our school teacher gave on how to become a millionaire.

God said "This is my beloved Son, and I am wonderfully pleased with him. Obey him." (Matthew 17:5)

"But now in these days he has spoken to us through his Son *to whom he has given everything,* and through whom he made the world and everything there is." (Hebrews 1:2)

"For his Holy Spirit speaks to us deep in our hearts, and tells us that we really are God's children. And since we are his children, *we will share his treasures—for all God gives to his Son Jesus is now ours too.*" (Romans 8:16-17) The King James Version says it this way: "The Spirit itself beareth witness with our spirit, that *we are the children of God: And if children then heirs; heirs of God, and joint-heirs with Christ; . . . .*"

Do you realize what these promises mean? Can you even imagine what God says? Do you realize this is a promise to each of us—personally, individually. It's not a trick! It's not phony! It's not abstract! It's not impossible! It's genuine, real, and for anyone who wants it! But we must *want* God and Jesus completely, more than anything else or all things combined in this world. We must seek God's ways with all our hearts. We must be

3

willing to follow each instruction given by Jesus for the rest of our lives. We must dissolve all partnerships with ourselves, things or Satan; we must dispose of all stock we have in ourselves—sell out completely. Then—it's a free gift.

For thirty one years I read these promises. I knew they would come true in heaven. I felt God would help me in my business, and in many ways he did. Yet I never really tapped into the rich treasures God has for us on earth until I was about forty-eight. Only God can open each of our eyes to this magnificent availability of our unlimited heritage. I have prayed that as I share how I reached this Garden of Eden others can find this fantasy made real. It's so very simple—yet requires a total release of ourselves to the possession and control of God. It requires us to believe Jesus is real, is the Divine Son of the Almighty God of heaven and earth, and has complete control of everything, everywhere. That he wants to control us, but cannot unless we relinquish everything to him. We must WANT to obey everything he tells us to do without a single exception. What a fantastic, unfathomable privilege to be his servant and be privileged to live—not only with him, but in him—and to have him live in us and through us. Think of it—we are the Temple or "Home" where God and Christ Jesus live on earth.

What is the value of our heritage as a child of God? God actually loves us as much as he loves Jesus. (John 17:23) He gave everything to Jesus, including all the tangible and intangible assets in heaven and earth. He gave Jesus all of his power, his wisdom and glory. When we do what Jesus wants, he gives us the use of all that God gave him. I never dreamed nor imagined he meant all these promises can come true in the lives of ordinary twentieth century people on earth. It's strange that all those years I really didn't believe God.

I want to go farther and farther into exploring, living in and working in this overwhelming Kingdom of God. I've enjoyed the past few years since I first entered this modern day promised land, and each new discovery excites me more than the ones before! Frances and I have seen Jesus do such fantastic miracles by the power of God's Holy Spirit that we can hardly believe what we see.

When a large lump on a body instantly ceases to exist before our very eyes because of the touch of Jesus, we come a little nearer to comprehending what happened when Jesus "spoke the universe into existence." And just as he spoke the universe into existence, he can speak success into our business, our marriage, our home or place in society—our everything!! If we WANT him to, and if we *WANT HIM!*

The "growing" pains and joys of my search for all of God in my life still goes on. It will until I reach heaven. "Don't cause the Holy Spirit sorrow by the way you live. Remember, he is the one who marks you to be present on that day when *salvation from sin will be complete.*" (Ephesians 4:30)

The abundance God gives while he is making room for himself in us is so exciting and marvelous, that his corrective discipline becomes less noticeable—and less necessary. Every minute of life overflows with inner peace and joy as we learn to walk, talk, think and act in the Spirit while journeying through life on earth to our home in heaven!

Follow me through these next pages as I have followed Jesus—and see his glory made available for each of us—NOW!!!

THE WORLDS BEYOND

I'm writing this chapter in a beautiful setting on the banks of the Black River with wooded hills as backdrops in LaCrosse, Wisconsin. We have the joy of seeing just about all the scenic wonders of our nation from the air, ground and water. We see and marvel at God's handiwork and man's accomplishments in molding and shaping the putty provided at creation into buildings for business or beauty or both. Our earth is magnificent!! "And God saw everything that he had made, and behold, it was *very* good." Gen. 1:30 (KJV)

The Microscopic World

In high school biology I recall the wonder of my first peek through a microscope. I had seen many drops of water before—sometimes one standing alone; sometimes raindrops falling by the thousands. But when I looked at that first ordinary drop through the enlarged eyes of a microscope I saw a whole new and different world. I was astounded and fascinated at the living world moving about in a small world that had been completely unknown and overlooked by me before. That was a lost world to me, but suddenly a whole new world—a universe— a galaxy had been discovered. And that world grew into greater dimensions as I looked at the new world of and on and in a tree leaf, a blade of grass, a grain of sand, a tiny thin hair, a segment of skin, or a smear of blood.

The Underwater World

Then one day I visited Silver Springs, Florida and discovered for the first time still another world. I had been on lakes and rivers hundreds of times before and had always loved to wade or swim or fish in mountain streams or the ocean. But underneath this water world seen through a glass bottom boat was the amazingly interesting and beautiful melody of balance of fish of all shapes and kinds, of bubbling springs blowing their breath to make the underwater seaweed and grasses wave like fields of grain weaving in the wind of that 'other' world outside. I could scarcely drink in enough of this additional new world I had stumbled upon—always existing, but not known or understood by me.

The World of the Bible

My mind floated back through memories to yet another world I discovered when I was about eight. Poppa (that's the way Mama spelled it) and

Mama were "saved" when a red-headed itinerant Baptist preacher came to the remote New Mexico village where we were homesteading. Jesus became real to them as they searched for his ways in the Bible. They had very little education, but God's Holy Spirit will teach anyone with enough hunger, discipline and willingness to accept the answers he gives. And teach them he did! They in turn taught me and I began to find exciting stories in the Bible and Bible story books. God soon created in my young undiscovered heartworld a desire to know him and his Word. This world, new to me, led my inquisitive mind to want to learn more. The tremendous love my parents had for us six children and the enormous love God *is,* caused me at this tender age to want to serve God all my life.

I memorized the Beatitudes (Matthew 5), John 3:16, and other familiar scriptures. My imagination would run wild as I read stories in the Bible. I spent hours living right along with Abraham, Moses, Jesus, Peter, James and John. Perhaps the time in history I would have most liked to live (except with Jesus) was right after God had finished creating the earth, the animals, Adam and Eve, and the Garden of Eden. What a perfect place that was, and even God walked in the Garden.

The valley where we lived wasn't like the Garden of Eden where I ran and played in my imagination. We did have a beautiful mountain river and acres of clover and grass meadows, shaded by huge cottonwood trees and willows, and I loved to play there. I herded my father's cows in the meadows. But up above the river bottom was where we lived and it was very dry most of the warm months after the snow melted.

A New World of Taste

Our summers were so short that tomatoes would rarely get ripe. We could not grow fruit at all. One time when I was about eight years old my brother Clyde and I had accumulated a big sum of money (a dime), and the carnival came to a town about four or five miles from our home. We walked over to see all these rides and games and things which we had never seen before. We enjoyed seeing them and like all kids, we wanted to do and see everything, but with just a dime between us, we had to do some very careful choosing. Want to know how we spent our dime? We bought six ripe bananas! We had never had one before. We went around to the back of a tent and ate them. I can taste them right now! I don't think I had ever tasted anything so good! We held every bite of them in our mouths and just let them melt slowly so they would last as long as possible. How I loved that first banana I ever tasted!

In the fall a neighbor family would go in their wagon way down south of us and come back with the whole wagon bed loaded with apples and pears. They always gave us a few pieces. I'll never forget the first pear I ever tasted! It was ripe and juicy and sweet and when I took each bite the juice would run out the sides of my mouth. It was so good I quickly licked it back, not wanting to lose even one drop. It tasted so delicious it always made me want more, but we knew we wouldn't have more for another whole year.

All of this made me appreciate the Garden of Eden world God created and you can see why I made so many imaginary trips to this land of abundance. I could retaste every bite of pears, apples and bananas as I read about the fruit trees growing along the river. To me that river was like the Chama River I knew so well, except it had all the fruit growing there.

It broke my heart when Eve and Adam ate the fruit God had told them to leave alone. I thought there must have been poison in the fruit because God said they would die if they ate it. Among all that fruit, why did they have to eat the one which was forbidden. I almost got mad at them because they were so stupid.

I saw how God made them leave the garden and go out into the dry land where thistles and thorns grew. My father worked land like this and it was really hard for us to hoe out thistles from our gardens and corn fields. They would stick and hurt if you tried to pick them up to burn them.

I had to help irrigate, too, and that was hard work. I was little, and when mud stuck to the hoe or shovel used to make dams to cause the water to run where it was supposed to, they got heavy and I got awful tired. But when I got tired that didn't keep me from working right on, or the water would get out of control. I just knew Adam and Cain had to work like I did. They would have kept living in the garden and not had to work if they hadn't disobeyed God. And God didn't give them a lot of commands they had to remember. He didn't even give them ten laws—just one—"Don't touch."

We moved to Texas when I was twelve, and would you believe it—we operated a fruit orchard! Isn't that just like our God! We grew mostly Elberta peaches, sweet, juicy, and delicious! We had one tree in the orchard which was a different species. In our first season we watched the peaches as they developed until finally a few began to ripen. This "different" tree had much more perfect fruit and the peaches must have been more than twice the size of the Elbertas. We carefully waited until they were fully developed and completely ripe before we pulled the first one. We could hardly wait, but finally Poppa said it was ripe and ready. We took our first bite and—it didn't taste like a peach at all! In fact it didn't taste like anything. We could have eaten cardboard with as much flavor. What a terrible disappointment this was!

When I thought of Adam and Eve tasting their first bite of that Garden of Eden fruit God commanded them not to eat, it reminded me of our big disappointment. Eve must have been enticed and enthralled by the physical appearance of that "different" fruit. But oh, how disappointing it was to her and Adam. The after-taste must have at first been very bland and then it must have become bitter. Satan still uses the same tactics. Sin looks so good and promises so much, but it always ends in a total disappointment.

These were exciting childhood and early adult worlds. I have always had an inquisitive, searching mind. This has resulted in my constantly looking into meanings of spiritual truths since I met Jesus, searching out the hidden mysteries of principles of life so often hidden under rocks of man-made doctrines, or behind walls of denominationalism, or hidden because we don't search beyond our complacent known world of religion.

The Spiritual World

How are spiritual worlds hidden from our view and yet seen by others? Look at John 12:35-41.

[35] Jesus replied, "My light will shine out for you just a little while longer. Walk in it while you can, and go where you want to go before the darkness falls, for then it will be too late for you to find your way. [36] Make use of the Light while there is still time; then you will become light bearers."[e] After saying these things, Jesus went away and was hidden from them.
[37] But despite all the miracles he had done, most of the people would not believe. he was the Messiah. [38] This is exactly what Isaiah the prophet had predicted: "Lord, who will believe us? Who will accept God's mighty miracles as proof?"[f] [39] But they couldn't believe, for as Isaiah also said: [40] "God[g] has blinded their eyes and hardened their hearts so that they can neither see nor understand nor turn to me to heal them." [41] Isaiah

was referring to Jesus when he made this prediction, for he had seen a vision of the Messiah's glory.

I continually search through the Bible for new, exciting and meaningful revelations from God—not big theological knowledge—just simple thoughts from God which give more understanding of ways to please him.

Recently a pastor received the baptism of the Holy Spirit as we ministered in the front of his church. We were guests in his church where he had been pastor for many years. God led us to announce to the congregation immediately after he had received the baptism that those who were sick or afflicted were to come to him for prayer instead of to us. We asked Jesus to anoint his hands for the healing of the sick.

He had only discovered a month or two before that people were being healed in the twentieth century. Obediently he prayed for the first person who came with a shoulder problem and pain. Instantly she was healed and pain left! He stood amazed, looking at his hands! He prayed for another who was healed! Then another—and another! Within about thirty minutes he had watched Jesus touch and heal about thirty people—almost everyone he touched! He could not believe this was happening—especially not through him.

He began to comprehend what was meant by Jesus living in and through a human. When we were alone with him after the meeting he said

14

"How could I have been a minister 36 years and never even know of this Power?"

He had discovered a new world—a spiritual world of Power—the real kingdom of heaven on earth!

The World Beyond Our Intellect

Let me share just a little of a discovery of the world beyond our intellect—the world Jesus wants us to find and live in while we are here on earth.

One day Frances and I were riding in a car in north Michigan. She and the lady driving were talking, and my mind, relaxed by the beautiful fall colors of the trees, began thinking to God. My thoughts went something like this: "Father, you placed such great importance all through the Bible on the 'first' son of Old Testament families, the 'first' fruit to be given to you—even Jesus is your 'first' son."

The "first" miracle Jesus did on earth was turning water into wine. Why was this his first miracle and what is the spiritual meaning of it? Why was it important enough to be "first?"

God flashed a whole series of scriptures and stories into my mind—like a picture seen all at once! It was not like a row of words that became a sentence and then paragraphs; and yet the thoughts were in sequence. This is what he said: "In a communion service we partake of bread and wine." I knew the bread represented the body of Jesus to be eaten in remembrance of him, and the wine was a token of God's new agreement to save us—an agreement sealed with Jesus' blood poured out to purchase our souls.

"Blood is life. Wine represents life-blood." Then God said the "first" thing we must do to be a Christian is to be saved, to be born into the Kingdom of Heaven. Then the third chapter of John flashed into my mind. Look at it carefully, verses 1-8:

3 AFTER DARK ONE night a Jewish religious leader named Nicodemus, a member of the sect of the Pharisees, came for an interview with Jesus. "Sir," he said, "we all know that God has sent you to teach us. Your miracles are proof enough of this."

³ Jesus replied, "With all the earnestness I possess I tell you this: Unless you are born again, you can never get into the Kingdom of God."

⁴ "Born again!" exclaimed Nicodemus. "What do you mean? How can an old man go back into his mother's womb and be born again?"

⁵ Jesus replied, "What I am telling you so earnestly is this: Unless one is born of water[a] and the Spirit, he cannot enter the Kingdom of God. ⁶ Men can only reproduce human life, but the Holy Spirit gives new life from heaven; ⁷ so don't be surprised at my statement that you must be born again! ⁸ Just as you can hear the wind but can't tell where it comes from or where it will go next, so it is with the Spirit. We do not know on whom he will next bestow this life from heaven."

Notice verse 5 "unless one is born of *water*"—this is when we are born physically; "and the *Spirit*"—this is when we are born spiritually, we cannot enter the Kingdom of God. Then in verse 6 "Men can only reproduce human life, but the Holy Spirit gives new life from heaven." We must be turned from Water into Wine—from physical to spiritual life. We are already *WATER* (born physically) but we must be turned into *WINE* (Holy Spirit given life). We must be born again! That's why Jesus' first miracle in our spirit-life must be the same as his first miracle on earth!

+ + +

Jesus died - to live
We die - to live
Grain of wheat - dies to live

The World of Abundance

During the six months following Frances' and my receiving the baptism of the Holy Spirit, the desire to know Jesus in a more personal, intimate way grew in me. We both spent every available minute in baptizing our minds, our souls, and our spirits with the written Word of God.

The more we read the more we wanted to read; the more of ourselves we yielded to God, the more his Spirit called us to yield; the more we searched, the more we found—the spiritual realm of God's Kingdom is. a vast, unending dominion of great riches, all available for the spiritual prospector. In the book of Colossians, we found one of our favorite veins of gold—a river bed full of gold nuggets: "For God's secret plan, now at last made known, is *Christ himself.* In *him* lie hidden all the mighty, untapped treasures of wisdom and knowledge." (Col. 2:3)

... "For in Christ there is all of God in a human body; so *you have everything when you have Christ,* and you are filled with God through your union with Christ. He is the highest Ruler, with authority over every other power." (Col. 2:9-10)

One day I was thinking to God and my thoughts went something like this: "Father, you know I love Jesus far more than I even love Frances. Yet, Father, I feel her presence and see her more clearly than I do him. How can I know and be so close to Jesus that he will be even more real and alive to me than my beloved Frances?"

God answered so beautifully as he "thought" back to me by flashing upon my brain a message. I quickly recognized this as the Holy Spirit speaking to me and I began developing the exposure he placed on my brain in a single picture. He reminded me of Saul on the road to Damascus to persecute the Christians. Saul had been a religious leader. He had never met Jesus and did not believe him to be the Messiah, the divine Son of God. But that day Saul met Jesus personally and was wholly his servant the rest of his life on earth.

Paul wrote a great part of the New Testament, telling us clearly and intimately about Jesus. God's Spirit put the thought into my mind "Where did Paul learn this much about Jesus—not in the New

Testament because it had not been written; it had to be in the Old Testament." God reminded me that Paul was taught by the Holy Spirit as he studied the then written scriptures. God said to me, "You go back to the Old Testament and I'll show you Jesus who has lived since the beginning."

I immediately began a new, exciting search for Jesus in the Bible. Remember how Jesus taught by using examples of physical things people understood, but making spiritual applications—he called them parables. In the 13th chapter of Matthew, for example, he told about a hidden treasure, a pearl of great value, or a farmer sowing seed, the wheat and thistles, and many others. He made the people angry because they couldn't understand what he was talking about—and he didn't intend for them to know because they hardened their hearts against him. The Holy Spirit of God reveals the hidden spiritual truths of these surface illustrations to those who believe. Jesus said in John 14:23: "I will only reveal myself to those who love me and obey me."

I started at the beginning of the Bible and when I reached Genesis 2:8-10, it seemed like I suddenly broke through the surface of the earth and saw a new world underneath the crust of the earth. It was like discovering the other worlds through a microscope, a glass bottom boat, and Bible stories. As a child I would imagine myself in the jungles of darkest Africa, moving through the thick undergrowth, hacking away the heavy foliage with a machete knife and suddenly reaching a big opening to come upon the original Garden of Eden—just like it was when Adam and Eve lived there. This time I discovered a spiritual world just below the crust of the physical world I had previously admired so much:

"Then the Lord God planted a garden in Eden, to the east and placed in the garden the man he had formed. The Lord God planted all sorts of beautiful trees there in the garden, trees producing the choicest of fruit. At the center of the garden he placed the Tree of Life, and also the Tree of Conscience, giving knowledge of Good and Bad. A river from the land of Eden flowed through the garden to water it; afterwards the river divided into four branches."

I looked for Jesus and found him! "The Tree of Life" right in the middle of the perfect world God had created! A tree is the source of life for the branches and leaves. Jesus is the source of our life—eternal life. Other descriptions of Jesus stored in my mind by the Spirit came into focus:

Jesus said: "I am the Way—yes, and the Truth and the *Life*. No one can get to the Father except by means of me." John 14:6.

Like a tree was the Vine—Jesus said in John 15:1-8. "I am the *Vine,* and my Father is the Gardener. He lops off every *branch* that doesn't produce. And he prunes those branches that bear fruit for even larger crops. He has already tended you by pruning you back for greater strength and usefulness by means of the commands I gave you. Take care to *live in me, and let me live in you.* For a branch can't produce fruit when severed from the vine. Nor can you be fruitful apart from me. Yes, I am the Vine; you are the branches. Whoever lives in me and I in him shall produce a large crop of fruit. For apart from me you can't do a thing. If anyone separates from me, he is thrown away like a useless branch, withers, and is gathered into a pile with all the others and burned. But if you stay in me and obey my commands, you may ask any request you like, and it will be granted! My true disciples produce bountiful harvests. This brings great glory to my Father."

Just as the Vine is the source of life, so is Jesus the source of life. Jesus is described as the *"root"* of Jesse in Isaiah 11:10 and Romans 15:12.

Jesus, our source of eternal life, (the Tree of Life) is right in the center of the abundant world—his garden of Eden!! Glory!!!

And God even placed in the center of the garden the "Tree of Conscience, giving knowledge of Good and Bad." There was Satan, the snake, the source of everlasting death, tempting us with disobedience. God *wants* us to *want* him instead of Satan—his ways instead of our ways. Eve was given the choice of obedience and life (in Jesus), or disobedience and death (in Satan).

I noticed in the spiritual Garden of Eden "The Lord God had planted all sorts of beautiful trees there in the garden, trees producing the choicest of fruit." I said, "God, what is the spiritual meaning of all these other trees?" His answer came from his recalling into my mind many scriptures:

Jesus said in John 15:5 quoted previously

21

"whoever lives in me and I in him shall produce a large crop of fruit." Psalms 1:3, speaking of those (of us) who delight in doing everything God wants us to do, and day and night (we) are always meditating on his laws and thinking about ways to follow him more closely, David says: "They (we) are like trees along a river bank bearing luscious fruit each season without fail. Their leaves shall never wither, and all they do shall prosper."

But then came God's great disappointment—He had to banish man forever from the Garden of Eden. The abundance God had provided as a free gift was lost—forever?? God never wants to be away from His children—He created them to be his glory and to have fellowship with him.

Soon God spoke to Abram (Gen. 12:1-4) "Leave your own country behind you, and your own people, and go to the land I will guide you to. If you do, I will cause you to become the father of a great nation; I will bless you and make your name famous, and you will be a blessing to many others. . . . So Abram departed as the Lord instructed him. . . ." This was God saying, in effect— I am promising you another land of abundance, the land of Canaan, another Garden of Eden—a land where milk and honey flow, a land of plenty; and it's a free gift. It's all yours if you will obey me and will be the children I can love and nourish—and "spoil" with everything good.

God allowed the children of Israel in their centuries of journey to the "Holy Land" Canaan, to go into slavery in Egypt for 400 years. This was God showing what sin really is—slavery to an evil, harsh taskmaster, Satan. Then, just as God promised, he sent Moses as their deliverer, their savior. The struggles, pestilences and hardships were magnified when God chose Pharaoh to be the object of the display of his glory and power. Pharaoh's last act was to send his vast, well equipped armies after the totally helpless children of Israel. They were escaping until they reached the Red Sea. With their backs to the sea, no way to fight back, no way of escape, they became totally helpless and left to the mercy of an enemy who knew no mercy.

How very like Satan and his evil punishment he gives in exchange for man's volunteering to serve him. Sounds quite foolish, doesn't it? But God in his infinite mercy and grace and love for his own, "made a way of escape. Moses, their savior, simply stretched out his hand over the sea; and the Lord caused the sea to go back by a strong east wind all that night, and made the sea dry land, and the waters were divided." Ex. 14:21

It is interesting to me that the pathway of escape was a narrow path through the *Red* Sea. In the Old Testament temple in the Holy of Holies, the Mercy Seat was symbolic of the Presence of God, and the Ark of the Covenant was symbolic of Jesus. In the Ark of the Covenant were kept the laws, just as in Jesus we find our new covenant. No one except the High Priest could go into the Holy of Holies and he could go in only once a year to take blood as a sacrifice for forgiveness of sins. The people were kept from going into the Holy of Holies, God's Presence, by a thick curtain, a veil.

Now, just as a slit was made in the "Red" Sea for escape, so a slit was made in the side of Jesus for his "red" blood to be shed for our cleansing from sin. In just the way they pierced the side of Jesus, so was the curtain in the earthly temple split apart from top to bottom. Notice the pathways of escape from sin; of entrance into the Presence of God—by the Red Sea; by the blood of Jesus; through the split in the Temple curtain. And because Jesus became the Way into the Kingdom of Heaven, we can all go directly into the Presence of God, not separated by the veil of the temple, using the name of Jesus, our High Priest, as our admission. Hallelujah!

Once the children of Israel escaped from their slavery and were on the other side of the Red Sea, they could have discovered the Canaan land, their Garden of Eden, within a few days. They immediately began complaining, thinking of self. That's why Satan was thrown out of heaven like a bolt of lightning—he was thinking of himself; he wanted his way instead of God's way. The Israelites made a right turn instead of a left and spent 40 years in the wilderness, because of disobedience.

I had spent 31 years in a dry, thirsty, defeated life, trying to be a Christian my way, but finally finding my way into my Canaan Land when I gave ALL to Jesus.

When the children of Israel finally reached Canaan, it was a perfect "Garden of Eden," just as God had promised. This was the abundance provided for his children. It was a free gift. God promised to destroy all the enemies in the land

and give it to his children. They had only to obey God and they, just like Adam and Eve could forever live in this second beautiful garden of plenty. But just like Adam and Eve—they were given a commandment "For in the cities within the boundaries of the Promised Land you are to save no one; destroy every living thing. . . . The purpose of this command is to prevent the people of the land from luring you into idol worship and into participation in their loathsome customs, thus sinning deeply against the Lord your God." (Deut. 20:16-18)

Do you know what they did? They "nibbled in sin." They disobeyed God by preserving just a few lives to make their lives easier—"self" again.

Just look at what God promised: (Deut. 28:8-13)

> [8] The Lord will bless you with good crops and healthy cattle, and prosper everything you do when you arrive in the land the Lord your God is giving you. [9] He will change you into a holy people dedicated to himself; this he has promised to do if you will only obey him and walk in his ways. [10] All the nations in the world shall see that you belong to the Lord, and they will stand in awe.
>
> [11] "The Lord will give you an abundance of good things in the land, just as he promised: many children, many cattle, and abundant crops. [12] He will open to you his wonderful treasury of rain in the heavens, to give you fine crops every season. He will bless everything you do; and you shall lend to many nations, but

shall not borrow from them. [13] If you will only listen and obey the commandments of the Lord your God that I am giving you today, he will make you the head and not the tail, and you shall always have the upper hand. [14] But each of these blessings depends on your not turning aside in any way from the laws I have given you; and you must never worship other gods.

But again, just as with Adam and Eve, they were banished from a land of abundance, and it was lost—forever?? No, God continued to promise all he had taken away if they would only repent and turn from their wicked ways and obey his ways. "Come, let's talk this over! says the Lord; no matter how deep the stain of your sins, I can take it out and make you as clean as freshly fallen snow. Even if you are stained as *red* as crimson, I can make you *white* as wool! If you will only let me help you, if you will only obey, then I will make you rich! But if you keep on turning your backs and refusing to listen to me, you will be killed by your enemies; I, the Lord, have spoken." (Isa. 1:18-20)

Then God provided the third Garden of Eden for his children. Just as God had promised hundreds of years before, he sent Jesus, his only Son, to earth. God through his prophets had told in exact, intricate details, how to know Jesus and what he would be like. Jesus said in John 10:10. . . . "I am come that they might have life, and that they might have it *more abundantly*." (KJV)

GOD WANTS US TO HAVE A BEAUTIFUL HOME OF ABUNDANCE!!!

Three times he has offered:

1. The Garden of Eden
2. Canaan Land
3. Jesus

Jesus is the only way to abundance! And we can only reach the Kingdom of God through:

The Red Sea (the highway to freedom)

His Red Blood—"Heaven can be entered only through the narrow gate! The highway to hell is broad, and its gate is wide enough for all the multitudes who choose its easy way. But the Gateway to Life is small, and the road is narrow, and only a few ever find it." (Matt. 7:13-14) Jesus said "I am the *Way*—yes, and the Truth and the Life. No one can get to the Father except by means of me." (John 14:6) The Way in is like a needle, a gate, a door, a highway: Jesus has a standing invitation to us: "Look! I have been standing at the *door* and am constantly knocking. If anyone hears me calling him and opens the door, I will come in and fellowship with him and he with me." (Rev. 3:20) Only by being a child of God can we acquire eternal abundance. We still must make our own effort to follow Jesus, *an investment,* to reach abundance in God's Kingdom. We must *want* riches to find them in the business world and then act upon our desires to reach our goals. We must *WANT* God's ways before we can even start toward his Kingdom. We must *WANT* his ways so much that we are willing to completely eliminate and subordinate our desires in favor of his desires—at all times.

The World of Business

Let me share some of the instructions I received from "Jesus" which established the principles upon which I based my business and spiritual journey to abundant living on earth:

"Ask, and you will be given what you ask for. Seek, and you will find. Knock, and the door will be opened. For everyone who asks, receives. Anyone who seeks, finds. If only you will knock, the door will open. If a child asks his father for a loaf of bread, will he be given a stone instead? If he asks for fish, will he be given a poisonous snake? Of course not! And if you hardhearted, sinful men know how to give good gifts to your children, won't your Father in heaven even more certainly give *good gifts to those who ask for them?*" (Matt. 7:7-11) What an opening God has given us to acquire a vast fortune!!

None of us like to be forced into a corner to where we are fighting against forces opposite our way of doing things. None of us like for others to "make" us do what they want. We are independent and like our freedom to do as we please! God has a simple way of giving us that freedom at all times. Look carefully at this scripture to discover the way to peace at all times, and sure success in everything you do:

God said in Hebrews 8:10 "I will write my laws in their minds so that they will know what *I want* them to do without my even telling them, and these laws will be in their hearts so that they *will want to obey them,* and I will be their God and they shall be my people." "And if under the old system the blood of bulls and goats and the ashes of young cows could cleanse men's bodies from sin, just think how much more surely the blood of Christ will transform our lives and hearts. His sacrifice frees us from the worry of *having* to obey the old rules, and makes us *want* to serve the living God. For by the help of the eternal Holy Spirit, Christ willingly gave himself to God to die for our sins—he being perfect, without a single sin or fault. Christ came with this new agreement so that *all who are invited* may come and *have forever all the wonders God has promised them."* (Heb. 9:13-14)

God never fails to carry out every detail of his promises. If we will carefully listen to his instructions for each assignment, make notes in our hearts; then keep our eyes on the end results, we will never fail to produce the right answer—and it can be written on our hearts.

I "WANTED" God more than anything else in all the world and all things combined. That day when I said "God, take all of my life and make me spiritually what *you want* me to be," I meant it with all my heart. I had made up my mind to go all the way for God, no matter what it cost in earthly possessions. "Love the Lord your God, with all your heart, soul and mind." (Matt. 22:37)

It was God, by his Holy Spirit, helping me "WANT" him. "For God is at work within you, helping you *want* to obey him, and then helping you do what *he wants.* (Phil. 2:13) "I will put a *desire* into their hearts to worship me, and they shall never leave me. I will rejoice to do them good

and will replant them in this land, with great joy."
(Jer. 32:40) What land? Abundant land—Canaan!

How can we please God? Let him bless us! How
do we allow him to bless us? By blessing him first!
Recognize that he is God and wants his children to
have full joy and blessings—abundance. Jesus and
God both say often, in effect "trust me and obey
me." What does it mean to "trust" God and Jesus?
Simply believe they will do exactly what they say
they will if we meet the conditions. The basic
condition is to give them first place in our heart
and not make room for a second place.

When Jesus was talking in Matthew 6 about
trusting him for your needs, he concluded with
"But your heavenly Father already knows perfectly well that you need them, and he will give
them to you IF YOU GIVE HIM FIRST PLACE
IN YOUR LIFE AND LIVE AS HE WANTS YOU
TO." King David, a man after God's own heart
said: "For you are great and do great miracles.
You alone are God. Tell me where you *want* me to
go and I will go there. May every fiber of my being
unite in reverence to your name. With all my heart
I will praise you. I will give glory to your name
forever, for you love me so much! You are
constantly so kind! You have rescued me from
deepest hell." (Psalms 86:10-13)

If we can reach that point of not wanting what
we think is best, but trusting God because we
know his way is best, and then submitting to him,
we begin a life which can be a perpetual Garden of
Eden in our business and spiritual life. Mary,
perhaps made the most beautiful submission of all

when she was told by the angel that she, a virgin, would be conceived by the Holy Spirit to become the mother of God's Son, Jesus: "I am the Lord's servant, and I am willing to do whatever he wants." (Luke 1:38)

When God told me to go into his Word, and listen to no man and he would tell me what he wanted me to know, I wanted so much to obey him that my whole being yielded to his every word, and I was willing to say what Mary said: "I am yours, Father, and will do anything you want me to do!"

It was over those first several months of searching and submitting, seeking and finding, his revealing and my yielding that I came upon that lost world—my Garden of Eden! I found a joy that lasted through every situation; I found a peace that nothing could disturb; I found a happiness that went on and on; I found contentment in my life as I had never known, love that grew like an overnight mushroom but lasted like a rock!

The abundance of Canaan has been my dwelling place for about six years now and I love it—every exciting second of it. The more I learn about the vastness of this new world, the more excited I get. Hallelujah!!! It's a journey from glory to glory!!!!!

"And he pointed out to me a river of pure Water of Life, clear as crystal, flowing from the throne of God and the Lamb, coursing down the center of the main street. On each side of the river grew Trees of Life, bearing twelve crops of fruit, with a fresh crop each month; the leaves were used for medicine to heal the nations." (Rev. 22:1-2)

Fresh, delicious fruit—all we can eat—an abundance of any and all kinds of fruit! Just as in the paradise of that heavenly city, so can we living on earth revel in the fruit provided in our Garden here on earth! When we are possessed by the spirit of Jesus and of God, we are heirs to the Kingdom of God on earth. In this kingdom we have an abundance of the fruit of the Spirit.

"But when the Holy Spirit controls our lives he will produce this kind of fruit in us: love, joy, peace, patience, kindness, goodness, faithfulness, gentleness and self-control; and here there is no conflict with Jewish laws." (Gal. 5:22-23)

Right here on earth we can eat all we want of any of this fruit and never get too much and get sick. We can just stand on the river bank at the tree bearing "love" and eat, and eat and eat. The juices can just run out the sides of our mouth and the sweet nectar will get better and better and better! Then, full as we might seem, we can go right on to the tree bearing the fruit of joy! We have the capacity to continue forever eating this fruit. The more of these kinds of fruit we eat, the more we become like them and no doctrinal laws separate us from the other members of the body of Christ Jesus. "If you are filled with light within, with no dark corners, then your face will be radiant too, as though a floodlight is beamed upon you." (Luke 11:36)

From Genesis to Revelation Jesus has made abundance available to us. Look at the final victorious life in Revelation:

2:26 "To every one who overcomes—who to

the very end keeps on doing things that please me—I will give power over the nation."

3:5 "Everyone who conquers will be clothed in white, and I will not erase his name from the Book of Life, but I will announce before my Father and his angels that he is mine."

3:12 "As for the one who conquers, I will make him a pillar in the temple of my God; he will be secure, and will go out no more; and I will write my God's Name on him, and he will be a citizen in the city of my God—the New Jerusalem, coming down from heaven from my God; and he will have my new Name inscribed upon him."

Rev. 21 "Then I saw a new earth (with no oceans) and a new sky, for the present earth and sky had disappeared. And I, John, saw the Holy City, the new Jerusalem, coming down from God out of heaven. It was a glorious sight, beautiful as a bride at her wedding. I heard a loud shout from the throne saying, 'Look, the home of God is now among men, and he will live with them and they will be his people; yes, God himself will be among them. He will wipe away all tears from their eyes, and there shall be no more death, nor sorrow, nor crying, nor pain. All of this has gone forever."

WHAT ABUNDANCE!!!
WHAT A GARDEN OF EDEN!!!
WHAT A LAND OF CANAAN!!!
WHAT A JESUS!!!
WHAT A GOD!!!

In that city made of pure, transparent gold like glass, a city 1500 miles in the form of a cube, our heavenly home, we again find the Garden of Eden.

"Blessed forever are all who are washing their robes, to have the right to enter in through the gates of that city, and to eat the fruit from the Tree of Life!!!!!" (Rev. 22:14)

Just like the abundance given to the first man, so is abundance given to those who follow Jesus, the Tree of Life—the source and giver of abundance! Amen! Hallelujah! Praise the Lord!

JESUS IS THE CENTER OF ABUNDANCE!

JESUS SAYS, "COME, FOLLOW ME!"

TURN LOOSE!
The Baptism with Fire

Even as a young child I had ambitions to succeed in life. Maybe they were daydreams, but daydreams can become real when determination and application are fused together with discipline. Perhaps I didn't realize that when God makes a man, he molds him over a period of many years into the kind of a person he wants him to be. Since God created man, he must have created daydreams as part of his molding process. I can see now in retrospect many instructions God gave me during my lifetime. I didn't know they were from him. Father God, may I now say thank you, and may I give you all the glory for preparing my life to be a part of your kingdom.

One hot day when I was about thirteen, my sister, Frances, and I were hoeing weeds from under our peach trees. Frances said she was going to either marry a man from Denver or be an old maid. I said I was going to be a bookkeeper and work in a cool office. I didn't know what an accountant was, but that became my spoken decision to follow that profession. Miracles often come into existence when the Holy Spirit speaks (or thinks) into our mind and we speak his thoughts with our mouth. God says in the Bible that salvation is confirmed by telling others with your mouth the Good News about trusting Jesus (Romans 10:10). I became an accountant and Frances became a "young" old maid before she married a man from Denver.

My life began to unfold in two main directions. I wanted reasonable success in business and I wanted to serve God. My attitudes began to develop and mold in a positive direction. I wanted happiness and discovered very early that happiness is found where you are now, and what you are now. I remember my mother telling my sisters that if you want to be a sweet old lady you must be a sweet young girl. My coach in high school, for whom I had the very highest respect and admiration, developed two deep vertical frown wrinkles between his eyebrows. I determined never to have such wrinkles from frowning—and I haven't. Someone told me it took 13 times more energy to frown than to smile, so I developed a smiling habit.

Attitudes are the inner person so I strove to develop and use positive happy ones. All sins are bad attitudes. All relationships to God, to Jesus, to our fellowmen and to ourselves are attitudes. If God stored forgiven sin in a heavenly warehouse and filed them alphabetically, he would use only the letter "A"—Attitudes. Of course, God buries forgiven sins in the deepest sea, never to be remembered again. Take murder, for example. The act of murder is an earthly violation of law, but it's the attitudes of hate, resentment, and greed which we develop in our inner being which cause the outward sin. These are the violations of God's laws of right and wrong. The application and development of God's ways in our whole life—our thoughts, our expressions, our actions, or re-actions—lead to a life of happiness and success. Love must be the foundation upon which all positive attitudes are built, and Jesus must be the cornerstone of the building.

I was talking to a successful young businessman recently who had found a form of peace in his business life. A few years ago his reaction to business pressures brought him ulcers and nervous tension. It was his medical doctor who changed his pattern of inner living. The doctor wisely coun-seled him to do his very best in everything he did, and then not worry about it. The young salesman clearly heard not only with his ears, but with his mind. As he traveled between cities, he meditated on clearing his mind of the attitudes of frustration, fear, worry, and negative forces. He discovered a form of peace came to him which allowed content-ment to mix with ambition. He discovered his work brought greater success, his mind had peace and clarity, his body became healthy. That is fantastic!

But real peace was just beyond where he was. He had not found the genuine peace that only comes when Jesus lives in you and works through you.

As I talked to him about Jesus, I explained God made his laws at the very beginning of the creation of earth and man. God's laws are always positive, and when we obey them we discover they work—

even by non-Christians. The only problem is that non-Christians don't know how to apply these laws fully—this is revealed only by God's Holy Spirit in you. The devil's ways are always negative and when applied in our lives, they bring negative results—bad results—frustration, worry, bitterness, anger, and many others. These attitudes lead to eventual destruction of our minds, our bodies, and our spirits.

With positive determination I began to develop leadership qualities and constantly found myself in business and church jobs bigger than I felt qualified to do. Each time an opportunity came my way I jumped right in the middle of it and did the job I accepted. It took a lot of hard work and study. Never would I accept anything with the attitude I couldn't do it. I knew I could if I used my mind fully and my energies freely. Life became an adventure of pursuit and I enjoyed finding each new step up the ladder to success and happiness.

By the time I was eighteen I was youth leader in my denomination in local and state groups. Later I was Sunday school teacher, church treasurer, church host, member of the choir, and served on nearly every board and activity of the church. Outwardly complete in my position, but in a way I cannot describe, there was a void inside this energetic me. A lot of people considered me one of the finest Christians they knew. Actually, I was spiritually a dried-up prune!

Many thoughts came into my searching mind and some left me with just a pastel shade of guilt. I know now the thoughts came from God's Holy

Spirit, saying to self-righteous Charles—"be ye holy as I am holy." Charles kept "almost" thinking back to God—I am holy and not really sinning. I reminded God that not only had I gone to the altar to get "saved" but I had been there to get "sanctified," also. Being "sanctified" was an experience I had been taught was for God to remove the root of sin so you could never sin again. I never really understood this. I never found any real difference in my life when I was "sanctified" except my deepening mental commitment with a renewed determination to give more of my life to God. It was really the Holy Spirit I needed. I tried to live without sinning. I never really committed any big sins. You might say I was a "sweet sinner."

I just couldn't accept the doctrinal beliefs of some of my friends. I remember one day I got so mad arguing with them about how right I was and how wrong they were. As I look back now I can recognize some of my sins: the attitude of anger (Gal. 5:20); arguing scriptures (keep out of foolish arguments—I Tim. 6:20) "criticism" and "feeling that everyone else is wrong except those in your own little group." (Gal. 5:20) God established laws to let us see our sins, and then he sent Jesus to earth to cause us to "want" to obey him, and to forgive our sins.

When I was thirty-five an evangelist led a revival in our church. One night he preached a sermon on discipleship and the Spirit of God began to deal with me about my state of complacency (of being luke-warm) and about giving all to God. This is what I wanted and what I needed. I was on the back row of the choir. We were singing "I surrender all." Thoughts began to go through my mind about my shortcomings. I was approaching a decision which could affect my whole life. My thoughts went something like this: "Father, I'm already financially giving about 13% of my income—but if you want me to, I will try to give 13½% or maybe 14%. God, I'm studying my Sunday school lessons a lot, but I'll get up an hour earlier on Sunday and study more; Father, I'll visit my absentees more to make my class grow."

Our pastor and a few members of the church had been to a retreat of an organization called "Camps Farthest Out." They came back really turned on and shared some of the things that went on. It seemed rather emotional to me—more than I liked. I was concerned that our church would maintain a dignity where I could invite even business friends without being embarrassed. They talked about some sort of a silly little dance they did, called "devotions in motions." I felt like they should come down from the clouds and get back to earth where they belonged. I got the feeling they thought they were better than me. I'm sure if I attended such a meeting now I would realize they were very close to God and were really blessed by his Presence (and were better than I).

I realized that if I gave everything to God, he would do something different with me. I knew I would have to obey whatever he said. God knows how to find the unsurrendered part of our lives. I'm sure he was the one who put the next thoughts into my mind. "What would I do if I had to go to one of those retreats where I might get emotional and be involved in that silly dance? That seemed like a counterfeit act to me." I said in my thought, "God, I'd even do that if you wanted me to." Then, with God still going deeper into my heart, I thought: "Jeanne (my wife then, now deceased) is more against that kind of 'artificial' emotionalism than I am. If I'm active she won't go along with me! This will make her real unhappy!" I didn't want that to happen! So I just turned off my thoughts!!!

What had I done! I knew the first commandment was "Thou shalt put no other gods before me." I had, by refusing to put God before the desires of my wife, placed her as a god before the only true God.

For about twelve more years God left me in the desert of defeat in my Christian life. I continued to work hard for my church all those years, but being a carnal "Christian" is not too pleasant.

Finally in early 1968 we changed to a large, new church with about 3400 members. We had always attended a small church. We joined the fantastic choir and soon were settled in a whole new environment. We found love and friendliness among the pastors and congregation.

Jeanne rather suddenly developed a large tumor which ultimately led to her death from cancer. We did not suspect cancer at that time and felt an operation would solve the problem with no great danger. Neither of us was concerned. Then God really began to move in the spiritual part of my life!

41

It happened in May of 1968. There was no great sermon—No song of surrendering all—No emotions! A small group of men of the church had met, as we did weekly at 6:45, for coffee, do-nuts and chatter about sports and other events of common interest. We went into the sanctuary of the church where one of the men gave a short devotional talk, then we went to the altar of the church where we silently prayed before going to our various trades and professions. I liked this plan of men starting their day with their minds on God. This particular day seemed no different than any of our other meetings, and probably wasn't to anyone else, but it was to me! As I walked the few steps to the altar there was a tremendous drawing to God like a powerful heavenly magnet!

It reminded me of the manned rocket we had sent to the moon, but which had malfunctioned. There was great concern that it would not successfully return to the earth, and that the astronauts would be lost. When it was near the half-way point between the moon and earth, it was moving at a comparatively slow speed. Then it began to move into the powerful gravity pull of the earth. Its speed increased the closer to earth it came and finally at about 25,000 miles per hour it burst into the earth's atmosphere and they were home safe!!

As I knelt to pray, with no one knowing my heart except God and me, I silently cried out to God: "Take *all* of my life and make me spiritually what *you* want me to be. Take all of Jeanne's life spiritually and make her the person you want her to be." I continued praying— and a new thought came into my mind: "Even if you have to take her life physically!" I meant every word! When I said it I turned loose of Charles Hunter.

You would be absolutely amazed at what God did in my life the next four months!

NOTHING!

I went about my business life and church life just as I always had. I asked God to take all of my life—not just a little more of my money, a little more of my time, or more of my abilities. I asked him to take it all, with no terms or conditions on my part. I didn't try to tell him what I would do; I waited for him to tell me!

About four months later God gave me my first instructions. How vividly clear he said "Go into my Word and listen to no man, and let *me* tell you what I want you to know." I don't even remember how he spoke, but I vividly remember what he said. As I picked up my Bible, a Revised Standard Version, I simply said to God, "Tell me what you want me to know and I'll do anything you say." Thus began a transforming period of my life! I had such a burning desire to receive his instructions that I spent every minute I could make available, night and day, reading the Bible. If I woke up at 3:00 o'clock in the morning I got up and read as long as I could stay awake. Within one year I had meditated in God's Word more than 2,000 searching hours. Each minute was a personal talk with God. As he revealed to me, I yielded to him! He changed my attitudes, my desires, my whole purpose in life! I no longer wanted anything except to follow Jesus!

Always before I had read the Bible for two reasons. One was to learn the Bible so I could teach my Sunday school pupils all that I knew. Later I discovered God said, "Seek *me* and you will find me." He *is* Wisdom and Knowledge. The other way I used to read was with a "thousand" critical fingers pointed to other people, proving to my satisfaction with scripture that their religion was wrong. I could pick apart just about anyone in our church to prove they were not what I thought they should be. But when God told me to go into his Word and listen to no man so he could tell me what he wanted me to know, I felt one great big finger of love pointing straight at me! No longer did I read the Bible critically. It was just God talking hour after hour to a son he loved. I paid no attention to other people who lived now or who had lived when the Bible was written. I only wanted to know all he wanted me to know, and I only wanted to do what he wanted me to do! I began to see God's glory and his wonderful wisdom. He began doing many little miracles in my life as I shared daily at every opportunity what he had done. God's abiding Presence and constant personal attention to every tiny detail of my life had become a reality, and I loved every minute of it!

One Saturday while Jeanne was sick as I sat in the hospital reading the Bible, I came to the 14th chapter of Luke, the 25th through the 33rd verses. As I read these verses I felt Jesus was saying something to me that I didn't fully comprehend. I read it again and still I felt there was something more. All day long for perhaps over eight hours I searched those nine verses. As I read, "if anyone comes to me and does not hate his own father and mother and wife and children and brothers and sisters, yes, and even his own life, he cannot be my disciple," I said, "I don't understand what you mean when you say I must *hate* all those you mention in order to be your disciple." I said, "Jesus, you have no hate within you and God has no hate; I know you don't want me to hate anyone, so what do you mean?"

I searched for the meaning of the 27th verse, "Whoever does not bear his own cross and come after me, cannot be my disciple." Then he talked about counting the cost before building a tower. The depth of the meaning of the last of these verses didn't seem to reach me where he talked about a king asking for peace instead of going into a war he might lose, and then saying, "So, therefore, whoever of you does not renounce all that he has cannot be my disciple." I said, "Jesus, I have given you everything I know to give, and don't care what happens—I just want to be yours!"

After hours of searching I finally went to sleep, still not satisfied. The next morning was Sunday and I could read all day. I started by saying, "Jesus, I just couldn't understand the 14th chapter so I'll read on." As I read the first two or three lines, there was such a drawing back to the 14th chapter that I couldn't go on. Again I said, "Please tell me what you mean." As I read it again, his answers became clear.

As I looked at verse 27 it became obvious that

just as Jesus volunteered to carry his own cross to
his death for us, so we must be willing to die to
ourselves and our own desires for him. Paul said,
"It is not I who live, but Christ who lives within
me." In counting the cost I knew that no matter
what my clients, staff, or friends thought about
me, I had to do what God wanted me to do! Once
I made the choice to meet the conditions Jesus
made for discipleship, I must never turn back, even
if I lost all I had—wife, business, home. Jesus
placed the decision squarely and clearly in front of
me—all or nothing. He said that the greatest
distance of anything on earth is the distance
between hate and love. He made me aware that all
those people he named were people I loved most. I
prized them more than all else on earth. Jesus,
speaking to me by the Holy Spirit, simply said, "if
you really want to follow me all the way, you
must put your love for me as much above those
you love the most, as the distance is between hate
and love. Only then can I have first place in your
life." The instant reaction from my whole heart
was, "Yes, Jesus, I love you that much, and I want
to give all. I want to be your disciple!"

I remember as a child I was so impressed with
Jesus as he walked up to Matthew or Peter or
James and crooked his finger at them saying
simply "FOLLOW ME." In my young heart I
wished I could have lived back then so he could
have asked me to follow him. How I would have
loved that! I even wished I would have been with
him as he chose his disciples, as each one stopped

what they were doing and moved quickly with him as he just spoke "follow me."

Little did I realize that Jesus still "crooks" his finger, wanting us to follow him. Jesus lived in a human body called Jesus 2,000 years ago. Today he lives in the bodies of ordinary people who will give all to follow him as disciples.

That Sunday morning Jesus "crooked" his finger to say, "Charles, FOLLOW ME," just as clearly as he said it to Peter and the other disciples. I had no idea, no concept, of what he had planned for my life. I only knew I had to follow him!

JESUS DON'T SPONSOR NO FLOPS

The abundance of God's promise in Malachi 3:10 to open the windows of heaven and pour out a blessing so great I wouldn't have room enough to take it in, has been bountifully fulfilled in my business life as well as my personal life. It's like a never ceasing river pouring abundance from the windows of heaven. It's the kind of blessings that provide all there is to life on earth and in heaven. God himself offered this—he doesn't lie. He said try it! Let me prove it to you! He has!

My business motivation upon accepting the condition Jesus made for discipleship and the provision of abundant life on earth with him, was to listen for instructions from Jesus on how to conduct my accounting practice. I wanted only to trust him and obey him. That's all!

Let me mention again as I did in P.T.L.A.— PRAISE THE LORD ANYWAY, about the Spirit of God speaking to me. I had asked God for a little miracle one night when his Spirit spoke in very distinct, silent words, "Charles, let me do this my way!" Still another few minutes passed when I prayed for something else and again he said "Charles, let me do this my way!" Three times he said the same thing.

I thought he was referring to the condition of Jeanne. I had prayed for months for healing, but he was not speaking only of that! He was talking about everything in my life, including my business.

Jeanne had become very weak and needed more and more of my time. When I woke up on the morning of December 10, 1968, I knew that I was to give her desires and needs top priority over my business. I'm sure now it was God moving toward providing for my clients and for me in the plan he was to carry out in my life. My mind was clearly and peacefully settled by early morning that this would be carried out at any cost.

Let me take you back to the beginning of my business life to show you how God was guiding me, even then.

I never once veered from my decision at age 13 to be an accountant. I worked for an oil company, later a large consulting engineering firm, then into the U.S. Air Force, and following that, back with the engineering firm. My formal accounting education was spread over several years, but shortly after it was completed, I passed the state examination and became a Certified Public Accountant. Just prior to taking the examination I had been recalled into the Air Force for twenty-one months.

During that tour of military duty, much of which was spent in England, I considered three alternatives for my accounting career: 1. a large national CPA firm; 2. a major oil company; or 3. ... I could start an accounting practice with a CPA friend (we had discussed this possibility).

It seemed at the time that my imagination

might have been running a little wild, because I thought "suppose I start my own practice as soon as I leave the Air Force and my very first client is the mayor of Houston." I had no idea who the mayor of Houston was, but I knew he must be successful because Houston is big and being mayor is big business. Would you believe that within a few days after I returned to Houston, I became a partner with my friend and our first client . . . the mayor of Houston! The very interesting thing about this is that the mayor became my largest client and has been for over 20 years. Almost all of my work now is for this same family client!

Our practice began in two small office rooms in a downtown building. About a year later we merged our practice with another small practice and I became a partner with two other CPAs. This new firm conducted its practice in a residence converted into an office. We later built a small office building for our growing practice.

It was at this time that Jesus became a living reality in my life. A few months before Jeanne's illness began, we had decided we should enlarge our partnership by adding a young man and train him to become a partner to relieve us of our overload. This was accomplished by bringing into the firm a young man 26 years of age. Charlie fit our specifications perfectly. We brought him into the firm with the promise of a partnership position.

Within a few months after Charlie came with us, he introduced us to his brother-in-law, Dick, a CPA 30 years of age. We offered Dick a position with the firm to become a partner after a trial period. He wanted to enter a practice as a partner, but felt we might be restricted in reaching large new clients because of our location. He declined our offer, much to our disappointment.

Soon after that one of our clients told us that she was moving to the exciting new 22 story Post Oak Tower building in the exclusive Galleria shopping center. This was the heart of a large new commercial complex known as the magic mile circle. We investigated moving there. We were drawn by the belief that we would be able to enhance the stature of our practice by being in the new environment. We made the decision to move as soon as the building was completed, early the next year.

Charlie, very excited, had related our move to Dick and showed him the beautiful brochures of the new home for our business. Then came the morning of December 10, 1968, when I decided to give my first priority to Jeanne because of her illness. By 10 o'clock in God's wonderful timing, within two or three hours after this decision was made, I received word from Dick that he would like to talk to us again about joining our firm! When God instructs, he provides a way! "Before they call, I will answer; and while they are yet speaking, I will hear." (Isaiah 65:24) (That's speed!)

Dick had seen in our planned move the one missing ingredient in our firm, and decided to join us. We were very pleased! He resigned his position with the national CPA firm for whom he had worked about three years. His excellent experience in their income tax department made him a tremendously valuable addition to our firm.

Knowing I needed to be free of work during Jeanne's illness, I began shifting full responsibility of client's tax work and other financial responsibilities to Dick and Charlie. There was little time for training or explanations. They actually assumed about 90 percent of my work immediately.

Many of the clients had told me in past years never to send someone else to do their work. They wanted me to do it because I had become like one of their family and knew what they needed and was always enthusiastically willing and anxious to please them. It would have been very difficult under normal circumstances to transfer client responsibility quickly and completely to anyone else. I didn't realize how God was bringing about a future arrangement in a peaceful, orderly way, by using what seemed to be an adverse condition in sickness. Not only was he making it possible for me to be off work, but he was establishing a permanent release for me.

I love the way he does two or more miracles at a time. God's wisdom is so phenomenal! It's thrilling to realize he knows everything about everyone that has happened, that is happening, or that will happen. He, through Jesus, is in complete control of everything and brings about anything he wants to in his own perfect way. Actually Jesus is the manager of the universe and every detail that takes place in it. "And you (God) have put him

(Jesus) in complete charge of everything there is. Nothing is left out." (Hebrews 1:8) I can see plainly now how he so beautifully transferred a major portion of my work to Dick and Charlie and yet very adequately kept my clients happy.

The next time God instructed me was shortly before Jeanne's death when he told me to cut down to one-half time in my accounting practice. Again I don't know how he spoke, except I knew without a doubt he told me to do it. So sure was I of his instructions that soon after Jeanne's death I began putting his command into effect.

When he said to cut my time I could have said "But God, how can I take care of my clients when I'm already working overtime and have difficulty in keeping up with the work-load?" Or "How can I make a living by reducing my income that much?" Or "God, what do you want to do with that much time?" But I didn't say any of these things or even think of the consequences or reasons. I just obeyed God!

Faith is not so much believing for miracles as it is knowing you have correctly heard God. Jesus said "My sheep hear my voice, and I know them, and they follow me." (John 10:27) (KJV) "If you want me to protect you, you must learn to believe what I say." (Isaiah 7:9)

Simply by knowing, without a doubt, that I heard the instructions given by God's Holy Spirit I called a special meeting of my partners and staff. I told them God had told me to cut down to one-half time in my part of the CPA practice. He didn't say what he wanted me to do. I said I felt he wanted us to bring into the firm as future partners some young men, the very best in the accounting profession. They had to be experienced enough to carry the load of a partner, have a degree in accounting, either be a CPA or be one soon. We selected a minimum age of thirty-five. I felt we should pay whatever it cost to get the very best. There was no question raised about this arrangement. All concurred. When God gives instructions he also prepares the minds of all those concerned, whether or not they are serving him.

Some of my partners and staff were serving Jesus and some were not.

We asked Dick and Charlie to talk to their friends about joining our firm so we could expand our partnership by adding two more young men. We needed someone to take charge of our audit practice and another partner with heavy experience in taxes, but also capable of serving in any capacity needed.

During the next few weeks we interviewed several young men for the positions. Instead of being thirty-five, they were all thirty. They all had college degrees, majoring in accounting, were CPA's, had almost identical experiences, and were all seemingly perfect for our needs. They came one-by-one, or maybe two at the same time. References were checked and everything seemed ideal for each one to join our firm. We offered them a partnership position after a trial period. The young men each felt this would fulfill their desires to be in a growing firm as a part owner.

I had explained to each applicant during the

interview that God had told me to cut my time in half and I didn't know what he was preparing me to do but they were a part of that preparation.

After the partnership offer was made to each, I told them that God was putting together a CPA firm; that if he chose them to be a part of it they would be. I also asked God to block them if he didn't want them in the company. On that condition arrangements were made for them to give adequate notices to their employers and then come to work with us.

Amazingly, one by one they called back within a week or so to tell us they couldn't come for one reason or another. Either they received a better position where they were, a better offer was presented somewhere else, or some other opportunity they preferred opened to them. Each time I thanked Jesus because he had made it so plain that he was selecting the partners.

Finally Gerald came with us. Even at thirty he had over four and a half years experience as an auditor with a national CPA firm. He had been rapidly advanced into a supervisory position with them. He was exactly the one we needed and is so fantastic that he is one of the finest auditors in the CPA profession.

Then came Dan. Dan has a very 'mod' look, and is sophisticated. He graduated summa cum laude from Baylor University with a master's degree in accounting. He had been with one of the national CPA firms over three years and was rapidly being promoted. He is a CPA. His tax knowledge and experience far surpassed his years. His mind is so brilliant and fast that I am amazed how he can grasp with accurate decisiveness the complex meaning of tax laws.

This completed the firm as we supposed it would be with four young men added to the three existing partners, plus our staff.

My clientele was well diversified—doctors, lawyers, engineers, men successful in the building business, machine work, stocks, real estate, colleges and universities, and other commercial and industrial fields. These clients ranged from very small businesses up to the millionaire industrialists, from atheists to religious fanatics. For these several months as I worked with each one I shared with them in business conferences, private offices, shops or over a cup of coffee that God had told me to cut my part of the work to one-half. I told them I didn't know what he wanted me to do, but that we were bringing into the firm young men who would be working with them. I explained that we were bringing in the best young men we could find in the CPA profession and that I would be available when needed. God's Spirit walked before me to each one of these clients and not a single one had any reluctance. This had all been accomplished before the end of 1969.

In October, 1969 Frances was brought into my life and on January 1, 1970 at 12:01 A.M. we were married. The excitement of our romance and the interwoven series of miracles of God doing supernatural engineering to reconstruct our lives into his plan is told in detail in our book "MY LOVE AFFAIR WITH CHARLES." This book is unique in that we were sharing little "miracles in progress." We had written letters sharing the beginning of miracles, the end being unknown to us at the time. Yet because God was telling us what to do and say, the end of the miracles tied in perfectly with their beginning as the plot unfolded. The simple total trust of two people being fused together first in spirit and then in flesh was the "Big" miracle where God did it all. Yet it was after the wedding, during those first months, that the real miracles flooded our lives. . . .

Actually, every life should be and can be totally controlled by God through Jesus. This is the "normal" way we should live. It takes seeking and releasing to learn to "hear" him speak and then it takes a willingness to obey whatever he says.

Frances traveled on speaking engagements about half of the first six months of our marriage. We knew before we were married that God had given her this assignment and we were completely willing, even though our hearts cried as we so frequently were separated. I would have opportunities to travel with her occasionally. By the end of the 1970 income tax season I was going with her a little more often and sharing the love of God a little more in her public meetings. Actually we disregarded the financial cost of my travel expenses, contributing our personal funds to pay the cost. By the end of 1970, we had to put $5,000 into the ministry to break even but we were completely sure God intended us to minister together. He assured us that we could trust him completely to provide all our needs, but he required us to invest first. This principle is taught throughout the New Testament. Luke 6:38 says it so plainly: "If you give, you will get." Through 1971 we were invited as a team more and more, and God demonstrated his approval by paying all our expenses and giving back the $5,000. We praise him for continuing to provide our living outside the evangelistic ministry. To date we have not used one cent of the ministry money for our living. We understand somewhat the liberty this gave Paul who worked in a secular job to pay his way while he preached.

This began to take me away from the CPA office more and more. God was beginning to use part of the one-half time he told me he wanted.

I had been a partner in this CPA firm for about 20 years and enjoyed a beautiful business relationship with my partners. If a conflict of interests arose we simply discussed it and agreed on a solution and moved forward with great smoothness.

My oldest partner, nearly fifteen years my senior, had spent a long lifetime in public accounting as a highly respected, successful business man. His business judgment and integrity was a valuable asset to the clients he served. He knew accounting principles, tax law and other financial matters thoroughly and had always highly pleased his clients. He was more than a business associate to me—he was, and is, a personal friend I highly regard.

But, into our business family now came four energetic, ambitious young men, freshly inoculated with good college education and a lot of accounting theory. This was well seasoned by the experience they had in large CPA firms where new ideas and formats were being developed constantly. The accounting profession, especially in the audit field, was being nationally changed to meet the responsibilities being entrusted to and thrust upon the CPA's by bankers, mortgage companies and others who relied upon CPA's for their safeguard in the money market. They assumed their roles as partners and did everything possible to carry out the trust placed in them when they became Certified Public Accountants.

We "old timers" also were very conscientious and equally concerned that we fulfill all professional standards but young minds and those more seasoned don't always do things alike, even though the ultimate results are accomplished. We diligently worked on ideas advanced by the young partners to up-grade and modernize, if necessary or desirable, our accounting reports, policies, and procedures. By long hours of work, discussions, analyzing, scrutinizing, criticizing, legalizing, we would come up with a new format or policy; generally after compromising our habits to meet the new ideas proposed. Technically, at this time we three older partners had final authority in the firm on any decision.

After something had been agreed upon, I often would leave town for a few days on a speaking tour and leave all of my part of the company affairs in the hands of the young men. While I was away there were occasions when the other two senior partners would get to thinking about the changes agreed upon, and decide without further discussion, to go back to our "old way" of doing it. This had a tendency to irritate and discourage the aggressive young men, to say the least! When I returned they would tell me what happened and then somewhat in despair affirm that they had no voice in the business matters. The more I traveled, the worse this got until it began to be a very serious problem. They were even hinting that they were not willing to continue with these friction conditions of overriding decisions previously agreed upon. Something had to give!

God generally works with his created man in ways normal to the man. We are doing on earth the things we are doing because God made it so and he was pleased. God also never makes a mistake and his plans are intricately, precisely being carried out right on time. The sun rises so precisely on time that its exact second can be determined thousands of years in advance. And so it is with his plans for our lives—he knew long ago just what he would be doing with the life of Charles Hunter, yet in his never-mistaken wisdom he did not force me to serve him. I don't understand it, but I don't question my great, wonderful, perfect God—nor his way of doing his work. I love you, Father! Jesus actually chooses us—we don't choose him. Jesus said "You didn't choose me! I chose you. I appointed you to go and produce lovely fruit always, so that no matter what you ask for from the Father, using my name, he will give it to you. I demand that you love each other, for you get enough hate from the world! But then it hated me before it hated you. The world would love you if you belonged to it; but you don't for I chose you to come out of the world, and so it hates you." (John 15:16-19)

So that we can better understand what seemed like turmoil in this living story, and so that we do not have a tendency to point a finger at anyone saying "look—he's the bad guy, the villain," I want to share a Bible story familiar to almost everyone. This special meaning came beautifully, clearly into focus in a very disruptive period in my life. Maybe you can use it in your life, too, to be better able to give glory to God and to Jesus when things seem to go wrong. It also helped me to better understand that often quoted, little believed scripture in Romans 8:28 (NIV) "And we know that in all things God works for the good of those who love him, who have been called according to his purpose. For those God foreknew he also predestined to be conformed to the likeness of his son, that he might be the firstborn among many brothers. And those he predestined, he also called; those he called, he also justified; those he justified, he also glorified."

I want to share a little of the story of Joseph, the eleventh of twelve sons of Jacob as told in the Bible fully in Genesis, Chapters 37-50.

I used to love little Joseph, but I hated his mean brothers because they did such awful things to him. Maybe I felt a closeness because I had two big brothers who sometimes picked on me. (The good things they did far outshined the bad.)

Jacob was a devout man of God, chosen by God to fill his place in God's plan for his people. He was blessed in this position by much wealth as well as by a large family. In those days the father was the head of the family, even of grown, married sons. They operated as a business and were a separate unit of their community, working together tending sheep, cattle and taking care of their possessions.

God had a plan to carry out which would take many years. He chose to use the normal ways of man to implement this plan, but to cause situations to happen by his own power, as he wanted them to occur. That is a fantastic ability of not only foreknowledge, but of his absolute control of everything, even Satan, to make events happen as he wants them to happen, when he wants them to happen, to accomplish his desires. How simple it can be to serve a God whom we can trust to do all these things—just for us! Praise you, Father!

Joseph was Jacob's most loved son. This caused the other brothers to be envious. This jealousy flared up even more when Jacob gave Joseph a beautiful coat of many colors, and envy grew into bitterness. Some of the brothers did something wrong one day and Joseph told his father of their evil conduct. This further irritated them and their bitterness grew into hatred.

"When tempted, no one should say, 'God is tempting me.' For God cannot be tempted by evil, nor does he tempt anyone; but each one is tempted when, by his own evil desire, he is dragged away and enticed. Then, after desire has conceived, it gives birth to sin; and sin, when it is full-grown, gives birth to death." (James 1:13-15 NIV)

Because of this hate, the brothers decided to kill him; but instead a profitable deal seemed better and they sold their brother into slavery. He was taken into Egypt to become first a slave of an army officer, then a prisoner, then finally into Pharaoh's palace where he became the richest, most powerful man in all Egypt, except Pharaoh. God used a dream of Pharaoh to place Joseph in this exalted position, and used the fulfillment of the same dream to bring seven years of plenty followed by seven years of famine in not only Egypt, but also in Canaan where Joseph's family lived. Through famine and hunger Joseph's brothers, who committed the horrible sin of selling him into slavery and deceiving their father, were brought before him. Joseph put his silver cup and money into their grain sacks to establish enough evidence against them to put them to death, and he had the power to do this. The brothers knew their lives were in danger. But Joseph loved his family. After they had bowed before him, Joseph revealed who he was and it really shocked them. Not only did he have power to take their lives, he had by human standards good reasons to do so.

^{3} "I am Joseph!" he said to his brothers. "Is my father still alive?" But his brothers couldn't say a word, they were so stunned with surprise.
^{4} "Come over here," he said. So they came closer. And he said again, "I am

Joseph, your brother whom you sold into Egypt! ⁵ But don't be angry with yourselves that you did this to me, for God did it! He sent me here ahead of you to preserve your lives." (Genesis 45:3-5)

After all my years of hating these brothers and seeing the horrible things they did, suddenly I discovered it was not their evil ways; it was God's way of placing Joseph in a position to save their lives. How thrilled I was to have the Spirit of God put a spotlight on the real meaning of that story: "I am Joseph, your brother whom you sold into Egypt! But don't be angry with yourselves that you did this to me, *For God did it! He sent me here ahead of you to preserve your lives.*" Jesus up-dated this story when he said in Matthew 10:39 "If you cling to your life, you will lose it; but if you give it up for me, you will save it."

Sometimes we don't understand God's ways of doing things but he is always right, and always looks out for those who love him. This one thing I knew, I had fully given him my life, my home, my business—my everything. I didn't understand at the time it was happening, and I'm sure my partners didn't understand either. Now I see the wonderful life-losing, life-saving business upheaval God did to put me (and perhaps them) where he wanted me to be. Now I am where Jesus wants me to be—a plan he had long ago!

Although at the time we were going through this my human body and mind took some shocking blows, I still some way knew God was in complete charge. I had peace when turmoil existed; I had security when my earthly security seemed to be in jeopardy; I had assurance I was flowing in the will and way of God when to others (and to me) at times what was happening looked like I was a traitor to my senior partner. He was approaching a time when he wanted to retire, or be able to if necessary. A significant part of this security through the continuation of the business was about to be taken away. This bothered me greatly at the time because he had been good to me in my hour of need, and now would I be able to perform in his hour of need? But God was giving the instructions and I was hearing them and obeying them, even when my own feelings of right conflicted with the drawing of the Spirit of God. I had all the security I would ever need; my income was twice what I ever dreamed it would be. I had a beautiful home. I loved my clients. I was very happy in my business and really there was no reason to change. If the young men couldn't adjust to our way of doing things, I knew I could find others to help me and I could continue in the beautiful, successful way it had been for many years.

But I realized there was a drawing by God to keep walking one step at a time to where he was taking me—and I didn't care where that was. I just wanted to follow Jesus wherever he wanted me to go. Paul used an expression in Acts 20:22-24 which perhaps describes what was happening to me: "And now I am going to Jerusalem, *drawn there irresistibly by the Holy Spirit, not knowing what awaits me, except that the Holy Spirit has told me* in city after city that jail and suffering lie ahead. But life is worth nothing unless I use it for doing the work assigned me by the Lord Jesus—the work of telling others the Good News about God's mighty kindness and love."

Now, let's go on with the story of the accounting business—and see what God can do as we are led by his Holy Spirit.

Another problem beginning to mushroom was how my compensation could be adjusted fairly when I was more and more away on tours. What seemed fair to me didn't seem fair to my partners, and vice versa.

Problems kept rearing their ugly heads like snakes for us to try to stomp to death, but I knew God had said to cut my time to one-half and Jesus had said "Follow Me." I knew somehow, but knew not how, that Jesus would solve these problems. Paul said in Col. 2:6 "And now just as you trusted Christ to save you, trust him, too, for each day's problems; live in vital union with him."

Following several skirmishes between the young men and my other partners I returned from a lengthy tour and the "kettle was boiling." The young men said they had to talk to me right away, so we set an evening conference. They reiterated the problems of wanting to change to new procedures and report formats but were helpless. They had tried compromise, but when I was out of town even the compromised agreements were often canceled. They were debating whether or not it could ever work, and even were wondering if they should leave.

We worked for a long time going through the

procedures they wanted established, trying to find a way to satisfy the other partners. It seemed we were working against insurmountable obstacles.

About eight o'clock I spoke something that surprised me perhaps as much as it did them. I realized a little later it had to be a thought placed into my mind by the Holy Spirit. "Do you have any idea what would happen financially if the five of us took my clients, moved to another location, hired a secretary and started a new business?"

I had never before considered anything except remaining in the same partnership—why should I. I had it made there!

Now, look how God had been speaking to them.

"We didn't think you would even consider that."

"But do you have any idea what would happen?"

"Well, we took the computer runs of the past year's income from your clients and projected it for a year."

They had experience in doing planning and projection work for clients and they knew what they were doing. I asked them what it revealed.

"If we did what you said, at the end of the first year we (the four of them) would have to take a $3,000 each cut in pay; we would be $15,000 in debt—and (they gulped a little) that's before you draw anything!"

I had been drawing a substantial salary and would have to continue to do so. I looked at them and said "How much faith do you have in God?"

I knew that in my security trained intellect I would be an idiot to give up all I had worked for all my life. Here I was over fifty—should I exchange all of my security with retirement, sickness and death benefits and an excellent income I could depend on every month, for a new company? There would be inadequate clientele to support six people, the very probable incurring of debts, long hours of work without fees to build a new business and no promise of a cash income each month which I had to have.

When I said "How much faith do you have in God," inside I knew if we did this, it would be entirely on faith—not intellect.

We concluded our meeting and I called Frances to tell her I would be home in a few minutes. If you have read our book "How to Make Your Marriage Exciting" you will know that when I stop the car at home, I jump out and start running toward the back door where I find my Sweetheart with arms fully outstretched, waiting for me to love and be loved—THAT'S SECURITY!

Frances rushed to the car for an early greeting and an anxious heart to know what happened at the meeting. Our senior-high school daughter was right with her. We knew Joanie would soon be in college and were anticipating a substantial expense. I had already reduced my income because of my travels.

I explained to Frances and Joanie all that the young men had talked about, their problems and their desires. Finally I shared the discussion about a new business and told them also of the risk of loss of income at a time we had no adequate source to supply our financial needs—except we look to God as our source. He looks to us to do our best. I explained how I had climaxed the meeting by asking the men "How much faith do you have in God?"

When I asked Frances what she thought, without hesitation or word she simply raised her right foot and, as if stepping forward, put her foot down on the concrete carport floor. Instantly we knew God had spoken to both of us, giving the same answer to two people fully in one accord. Let me tell you how God prepared our minds for such sensitive reaction to a very important, major decision, and how we communicated that answer.

Moses had been chosen by God for a special 120 year assignment to lead the Israelites, God's chosen children, out of bondage in Egypt, through the Red Sea to their salvation and freedom and on into the Promised Land of Canaan. Moses almost successfully fulfilled his assignment, except for one disobedient act which stopped him just an eyesight away from his destination. God chose his assistant, Joshua, to complete the journey into the land of milk and honey.

A little over a month after Moses died, Joshua knew it was time to lead the Israelites across the Jordan river into their new home. He gave the command to the vast multitude of followers and they began to move forward. The priests led the march carrying the Ark. At the end of the first day they came to the river banks and there waited three days for their chosen day to cross. The river at that time was flooding, overflowing all its banks—actually impossible to cross. On the morning of the third day Joshua ordered the priests, "Take up the Ark and lead us across the river!" And so they started. They had been summoned to listen to what the Lord God had said: "Think of it! The Ark of God, who is the Lord of the whole earth, will lead you across the river! Now select twelve men, one for each tribe, for a special task. When the priests who are carrying the Ark touch the water with their feet, the river will stop flowing as though held back by a dam, and will pile up as though against an invisible wall!" (Joshua 3:11-14)

Now picture the priests leading this grand parade. They were carrying the Ark with poles through rings on all four corners, similar to the way a casket is carried today. I can see them, excited and anxious, on either side of the Ark marching toward the floodwaters with the Ark (depicting Jesus). They are at the water's edge. I can see the front two priests lifting their feet to place them into the water, just as God told them to do!

They could have at this point said "But God, you said the river would be dry!" But they didn't! They put their feet down, the waters dried up and they marched across the Jordan river on dry ground! *THAT'S FAITH!*

Frances and I had just read this exciting story and saw the faith they had to do the impossible, but to do it because they did not doubt God—and they did not doubt that Joshua had heard God speak and knew without a doubt what he said.

Frances and I were facing a seemingly impossible river to cross. God didn't say exactly how we would cross it or what was on the other side. We didn't attempt to figure out how he would lead us through the water, and we didn't even send spies across into the Jericho we were to claim as our own. All we knew was that Jesus assured us that if we would follow him, he would take us to a Promised Land, to an abundant life. We knew we could trust him to lead us wherever he wanted us to go, and with all our hearts we wanted to follow him.

Instantly when Frances put her foot down on the concrete floor, we knew the "water had dried up" and we knew God had spoken. By faith, and faith alone, our decision was made.

Early the next morning I met with the four young men, told them what had happened, how God had spoken and that by faith in God alone we were ready to go. And then I said "Have you the guts to go through with this?" I don't know if they decided by faith or by "guts," but we called a meeting of the other partners and informed them of our plans. I'm sure about then they felt like they were in the middle of the river, and were unsure whether the invisible walls of water would hold as we marched across.

Right then the atmosphere in our office was not exactly peaceful, and action began at once. For awhile I was glad the twelve men in the Jordan River story didn't show up with the twelve stones—they might have been thrown, instead of used as an altar.

We began to plan and negotiate the separation of my business from the total business. The overall plan was for me to take all the clients I had been servicing (identified as mine on our computer records), the accounts receivable and work in progress relating to those clients, the furnishings and equipment in my office and certain other office furniture, equipment and supplies. The cash and other assets and liabilities were simply to be divided in the percent of ownership. This sounds simple. I have worked with separation of other professional partnerships, and the division never comes out equitably because the dollar value and the list of clients don't match—not generally anywhere close, and neither does the feasible separation of furnishings and equipment.

But God can and does do miracles in today's business world!

We three original partners agreed on a method of evaluation of clients, furniture, and equipment. We felt an equitable valuation method for clients was to assume each one was equal to the previous year's fees. We made a list of every client. At the right of the client name we had two columns; one headed "Total" and the other "Charles." As we put values on the list, if I was to own the rights to the client business, we put the same figure in each column. If the other partners were to retain ownership, the value would be put in only the total column. When the entire list was complete and approved by each and all partners we totaled the two columns. It was a mechanical process and we had the ability to do that. But look at what God did while we were busy with the mechanics! I owned 43% of the total business. We were to multiply the total column by 43% and negotiate the difference between the 43% and the total value of my clients. Would you like to hear what God did? The 43% total and my client value were exactly even!! This would be like a million to one odds, but it's a sure thing when God does a miracle. This was just one of many ways God had of confirming his control of what was happening in my life.

To divide and evaluate the furniture and equipment, we did a similar thing. We made an inventory list of each item. Each of us took a copy of the list and put the value we felt applied to each item. We then agreed on a value for each item where our individual values varied. Finally we had set an agreed price on every item. This was put in the "Total" column. To the right was the "Charles" column. In this, we placed the value for each item we agreed for me to take. Then we totaled the two columns, multiplied the total by 43%. This list was several pages long, worth several thousand dollars, made up of some items over fifteen years old, some nearly new, and no effort had been made to equalize the percent value to the items to be mine. 43% of the "Total" column was only $200 different than the "Charles" column! And I knew the difference was not God's error!! Praise God!!

God continued to do many miracles and for each one I praised him and gave him all the glory. Too often we say "wasn't that a coincidence" or "lucky" or "nice," instead of quickly recognizing his miracles by saying "Thank you, Jesus."

Near the end of the year we moved to a beautiful new building in the same commercial area, hired a secretary and started our new business—on faith! By the time the details were out of the way, tax season was upon us. Any good CPA firm can keep busy in tax season and we hardly had time to look up until the end of April. The new partners rushed the computer report, projected it and the future work known to be available—and almost panicked! There wasn't half enough business to keep us busy the rest of the year. They called an after 5:00 emergency meeting where we really analyzed our financial plight. It looked very skimpy. Dan said maybe he should get an outside job and with that money, a lot of effort to bring in new clients, and with what we could do with our existing clients, maybe we could "poor-boy" it through till next tax season. I said no, that God had told us to start this business and he would carry us through.

Gerald searchingly said, "If we just had a $5,000 audit this summer we would have it made."

With a feeling of walking on thin ice, we concluded our meeting. I much prefer, and believe it safer, to "walk on water" toward Jesus, and simply trust him. Some day I hope he gives me enough faith to walk on physical water, but I'm thankful that he gives me many opportunities to figuratively walk on water through problems by faith—his faith, given to me like manna from heaven. And yet the miracles could not happen unless we stepped beyond our human capabilities.

And that's how we paid our bills for a while. When the rent came due we had just received the money a day or so before. When payrolls were to be met, the money barely arrived on time; but all payments were met on time by the manna God provided daily—enough, but none left for the next day.

After the meeting that night, Frances and I prayed. We said, "God, so that these young men will unquestionably see your glory and your miracle power we ask you to do a miracle and fulfill exactly what Gerald asked. We ask you in Jesus name to give us an *audit,* not a tax client or special project, *this summer*, because Gerald put a time limit on it; and a fee of *$5,000.*" We said "Thank you, Father," and praised him for what he was going to do. Then we added a P.S.—"Father, if you would like to give us more than $5,000, we sure could use it." He promises abundance, doesn't he? The next day I told Gerald and Charlie what we had prayed and to watch God answer.

We sincerely believe that if we give him first place, and all other places in our lives, he will give abundantly, financially.

About a month went by and we hadn't heard of any one wanting us to audit their records. Frances and I prayed again and I guess, in effect, we said

76

"Don't forget, God!" But God honors a sincere, seeking heart, and he never forgets.

It must have been the next day that I was in the office about 10:00 A.M. and my buzzer called me to the phone. It was Jesse, one of our senior staff men in the former partnership. After exchanging warm greetings, he said he had just left the employment of the firm and accepted a new assignment as assistant to the business manager of a large junior college in Houston. He remarked about my experience as auditor for several colleges and knew I was well established in college accounting, auditing procedures, and reporting. Then he said—"WE ARE CHANGING AUDITORS THIS YEAR AND WOULD LIKE TO TALK TO YOU ABOUT MAKING AN AUDIT!" To me it was the voice of God but it sounded to my ears like Jesse said it! I made an appointment and rushed in to tell Gerald—"God just answered our prayer—let's go get the audit!"

The short of the story was:

1. We got the *audit*—not a tax client or special project.

2. It was *that summer*, well on time.

3. $5,000???—$11,300!!!

JESUS DON'T SPONSOR NO FLOPS!!!

Business began coming in faster and faster and Frances and I were praying "God, we ask you to so supernaturally provide business for our firm until they can't keep up with it, so they can see without a doubt that you are doing it." Frequently I remarked to the partners how God was answering with more and more business.

I remember that fall, when normally work is the most slack, we were scheduled for a several day tour in Florida. The day before we were to leave, I was called to an emergency meeting. They said we were all so swamped and behind that they wanted me to cancel my part of this Florida trip. I asked if one of the clients I worked with was needing me. They said no, it's just that we were all behind. I remarked that for over twenty years I had promised God I would work for him as soon as I caught up my work. This rarely happened. I said, "No, I believe God has said to go, so I'm going. But, if a client calls and needs my professional services, I'll fly back to take care of it." I believe God will always see that we can do our secular job in a superior manner if we always do our very best. They were practically demanding and begging me to stay, but I believed with all my heart God meant for me to go. Finally, I said "Do you want us to stop praying for work?" Quickly one of them said—"No, no, no, don't do that!!!" Praise God, they recognized his miracle power.

The year soon passed, the records were completed for the year and we discovered the fruit of our first year in the new business:

1. The four partners did not take a $3,000 cut in salary—they made much more than they would have in the other firm.

2. We were not $15,000 in the hole. We not only had paid all bills on time; we had invested in some land syndications; I had drawn a substantial salary: they paid several thousand dollars to me

for purchase of furniture and equipment and other items, and we had a Certificate of Deposit for cash in the bank for nearly as much as we estimated we would owe at the end of our first year!

Along with these beautiful financial miracles came what was to me the most blessed bonus I could have received. Remember way back before Frances and I had even met God said to cut my work to one-half? In blind unquestioning obedience I never asked God what he wanted me to do with my half time. But during our first year in the new business, Frances and I had traveled the nation together sharing the Good News about Jesus and the love of God to multiplied thousands, working hard to do my accounting when we were home; and Frances working just as hard to make our bookings and answer hundreds of letters and do the other jobs of operating a growing ministry. I suppose we worked more than 15 hours a day, 365 days of the year. Would you like to guess my production time for the CPA firm? We knew it was difficult to produce 2,000 billable hours per year and do all the reading, administrative, and non-productive work. With only God planning the work-load, the computer showed my productive time to be 1,025 hours. Almost exactly half time! Thank you, Jesus!

Since that beautiful first year, the company has almost quadrupled in size. I have had complete freedom in traveling for Jesus. Frances and I work completely as a team and are never separated on trips.

The first of February, 1973, our book "The

Two Sides of a Coin" was released to the Christian book readers. This shared our head-on collision with the mighty Holy Spirit as we received the baptism of the Holy Spirit, just like the disciples did on the day of Pentecost. This launched us into a vast new world in our ministry. About February 15th God spoke to Frances and me simultaneously and said to reduce my time in the CPA practice to one-fourth time. I formulated a financial plan compatible to my reduced time in practice and the financial arrangement with my young partners. Before I could call them to tell them what God had said, they called me to a meeting where they presented a modified financial arrangement which they felt would allow them to expand more freely, and allow me to travel with less obligation to them. Amazingly their plan was almost identical with the one God had given to me. There he goes again talking to my partners before we can discuss his plan!! God is Fabulous!! On February 27, 1973, God literally dumped Frances and me into a miracle ministry where thousands have been healed physically as well as spiritually. This further expanded our outreach and more demand was made on our time.

I wonder what God would have done if he had picked a 31 day month instead of one with 28. Great is our God, and greatly to be praised!

WHO IS THIS MAN JESUS?
Jesus is the best CPA I know.

He is head of the largest business in the Universe—He runs the whole of heaven and earth—in perfection

He is our boss

He is our Master

He is our King

He is Everything we need to attain success abundantly—

"NIBBLING" IN SIN

God has been kept very busy showing me areas of my life which he needed to replace with his better way of life. Some came easily—others I had a more difficult time letting him remove and replace. But praise his holy name, he never gives up!

Jesus meant serious business when he defined discipleship. He meant for us to go all the way if we follow him. So many little things I had grown accustomed to doing were really not quite right or not quite true—almost, but not quite. I did a lot of "justifying" my little sins. The one who loses a race may be only an inch behind the winner—but he doesn't win. In high school I broke the county record in the mile race, but another runner was ahead of me at the end. God has repeatedly revealed little areas of "almost" sin in my life. I would hate to "almost" reach heaven. In my determination to be what God wants me to be, I have sincerely disciplined myself to quit sinning even a "little" bit.

Poppa had built lots of road beds and railroad beds with fresnos pulled by mules, so he was the one selected to build the irrigation system for the New Mexico valley where we lived when I was a child. I went with him and my big brothers one time up to where the water was to come out of the river. I really couldn't see how it would work. It looked to me like he had made the ditch go angling right up the side of a big steep hill and I just knew water couldn't run up hill. But I trusted my father and if he said water would go up that hill, I had faith in him to believe it would so I didn't try to figure it out—I just accepted it. What I didn't know was that the whole mountain was taller at one end than the other and the irrigation ditch was actually going down hill-up hill. IT WORKED! Since then I have learned that my heavenly Father does lots of things I don't understand, so I don't try to figure them out—I just accept them! I trust him and if he says a blind or deaf person can be instantly healed, I have faith in him to believe it. I even have faith in Jesus to believe he can manage my business decisions by using my mind to put the decisions into. It works!

Part of this irrigation ditch ran across our land. Along both banks of the ditch we had lots of clover and grass like it was on the river bottom land. Poppa and my two big brothers planted fields of alfalfa next to the clover which provided hay for our cows in the winter. My job was to watch the cows and keep them out of the alfalfa. If they ate green alfalfa, they bloated and would die if something wasn't done quickly. If they started to bloat, Poppa would make me run them around the corral an hour or two until the bloating disappeared. I didn't mind the running so much, but I couldn't have my supper till I finished with the cows. I knew I had better do a good job of herding—and I really did want to, but sometimes I got sleepy in the warm sun. My shepherd dog, Ring, would help me but he sometimes dozed off with me. It seemed like every time I turned my head, one of the cows' noses would be just in the edge of the alfalfa field. They didn't get all the way into the field, but they were always wanting to nibble in the alfalfa patch. That's just like a lot of Christians when they get saved—they want to see how close they can get to sin and stay saved and if they think no one is watching (especially Jesus) they just "nibble" in sin! Not much—just a little bit! It takes just a "little" bit of sin to make us spiritually bloat and this can cause us to spiritually die.

Do you remember the story in the fifth chapter of Acts about Ananias and his wife Sapphira? Read it and see what happened when they nibbled in sin.

5 BUT THERE WAS a man named Ananias (with his wife Sapphira) who sold some property, 2 and brought only part of the money, claiming it was the full price. (His wife had agreed to this deception.)

3 But Peter said, "Ananias, Satan has filled your heart. When you claimed this was the full price, you were lying to the Holy Spirit. 4 The property was yours to sell or not, as you wished. And after selling it, it was yours to decide how much to give. How could you do a thing like this? You weren't lying to us, but to God."

[5] As soon as Ananias heard these words, he fell to the floor, dead! Everyone was terrified, [6] and the younger men covered him with a sheet and took him out and buried him.

[7] About three hours later his wife came in, not knowing what had happened. [8] Peter asked her, "Did you people sell your land for such and such a price?"

"Yes," she replied, "we did."

[9] And Peter said, "How could you and your husband even think of doing a thing like this—conspiring together to test the Spirit of God's ability to know what is going on?[a] Just outside that door are the young men who buried your husband, and they will carry you out too."

[10] Instantly she fell to the floor, dead, and the young men came in and, seeing that she was dead, carried her out and buried her beside her husband. [11] Terror gripped the entire church and all others who heard what had happened.

I would like to share some of the areas in which I "nibbled" in sin until I was reminded by the Holy Spirit that they were not right. Also, I'll include "niblets" others have brought to my attention. Perhaps, if you want to walk with me toward discipleship with Jesus, some of these may remind you of the refining, polishing process which has taken place (or needs to) in your life. God's work on my life has progressed from the stage of chiseling off the rough outer layers, to soapstoning and fine polishing. He still has more to do on me—how about you?

"Nibbling" is trying to get by with what you know is wrong—and hoping you don't get caught (especially by God!).

In school it is so easy to let our eyes wander across the answer on the examination paper of the "smarter" student sitting next to us! Our "nibbling" started when we didn't fully prepare for the exam—maybe because we played a little too much while mother went to the store; or maybe because we were thinking of our boy friend or girl friend while we should have concentrated on our studies. Then the next "nibble" came when we first thought "I wonder what the answer is—I wonder if Bill knows; he's already completed that part. I won't really look, but just in case I notice as I look up, the answer just might come into my view." The next time you are tempted, just say "Jesus, I'm just going to sneak a peek—just a little 'nibble'."

In my CPA business I've had "honest" clients ask me "How much will the government allow me to deduct for donations on my income tax return?" I simply reply: "Whatever you have given." Some who wouldn't even consider robbing a bank are trying to gain just a little bit of savings by nibbling in theft—not much; just a little bit! It doesn't take but a few tastes of sin to entice us into the middle of the alfalfa field! Generally, if we feel we can get by with a little, we get greedy until we get caught. Even demons extend their operations too far and expose their evil existence.

Expense account padding can be justified if we want to sin—just a little bit!

It's nice to take just a minute or two more than is allowed at coffee break or during lunch time. "Nibbling" in sin?

"I've got three extra days of sick time I haven't used so I'll just tell them I don't feel good (I wouldn't want to say I'm sick). Well, everyone else does it, so why shouldn't I?"

"Mary, I'm going to be five minutes late coming back from noon shopping—will you be 'good' and punch my time card at one o'clock?" That time two of our cows "nibbled" in the alfalfa, didn't they?

I don't know if "playing hookey" from school is "nibbling in sin" or just plain sin!

We attempt to make sin sound sacred by calling a lie a *white* lie.

Have you ever let up on your job and just sorta took it easy? Not doing our very best for our employer is trying to get away with less than our best, when we would do better if we knew he was watching. Have you ever noticed how hard it is to keep working if the boss is on vacation or away from the office or plant? Remember, Jesus is actually our boss!

I remember one time our choir needed extra copies of the sheet music for a Christmas cantata. We knew someone with a copy machine and they were "nice" enough to make enough copies so that each of us had our very own copy—so we could worship Jesus! Were we worshipping Jesus—or Satan? That isn't really sin, is it? Yes—ask the one who holds the copyright and sells the sheet music.

Our teacher in school didn't allow us to chew

gum during classes or study period. I enjoyed chewing gum and just once I tried to get away with it. I hardly moved my jaws—but my teacher noticed. Actually, I noticed it long before she did, because I didn't like to do wrong—even a little bit. The Holy Spirit reminds us of right and wrong—even little wrongs, if we want to please Jesus.

I remember the first time I ever saw my two older brothers, Milton and Clyde, smoke a cigarette. It kinda shocked me but I wanted to be big and smart, too, like they were. In spite of all my begging, they wouldn't let me even take a puff. Praise God! But my attitude "nibbled." Neither of my brothers went on smoking. I have never even put a cigarette in my mouth, for which I give God the praise. I'm glad I was caught just before my first bite of alfalfa! No alcoholic ever took the first drink with the intention of becoming an alcoholic. We saw alcoholic young people on national TV recently. One of them said he took sips from bottles at home when he was five years old. He was an alcoholic before he was twelve! Most habits start by nibbling—just for kicks! Jesus says to present our bodies a living sacrifice, holy and acceptable to him. Only the holy shall see God. "Don't you know that you yourselves are God's temple, and that God's Spirit lives in you? If anyone destroys God's temple, God will destroy him; for God's temple is sacred, and you are that temple." (I Cor. 3:16-17 NIV)

I'm talking about wanting to be pleasing to God. Even our doctors will confirm that habits of tobacco, alcohol and drugs are damaging to our bodies. I don't believe Jesus would use any of them, and if we follow him, we won't either. You might be saying, "I don't see why I need to stop doing it." We have a saying at our house—"if in doubt, throw it out." We see thousands of Christians delivered of smoking. Some of them decide they'll test Jesus to see if he really delivered them, so they'll "sneak" a cigarette. Just nibbling in sin, and before long they're right back where they started from.

One afternoon I left my office for home. My mind quickly left my work and spent full time thinking to God as soon as I stopped concentrating on the day's duties. By the time I reached the elevator I was almost singing aloud about God's greatness. My office is on the 19th floor, near the top of the building, so I stepped to the back of the elevator as we descended. All of a sudden a sharp looking, well-built young lady with the most mini-mini-skirt you could imagine (you really didn't have to imagine much) stepped right before my eyes. Now you can't help seeing when something like that is the only object in your line of vision! Well, can you? I quickly turned my eyes in another direction so I wouldn't see what I had already seen. Just as I did, I thought: "I wonder if God saw me look"; then I realized he did (but I didn't want to admit it). He knew I couldn't help it! Suddenly I just looked up and said "GOD, DID YOU SEE THOSE LEGS?"

I imagine most men notice ladies' legs, their shape and exposure. It must be so, or else the ladies would not expose themselves. I had no desire nor intention to partake of the product advertised, but lust could have been fed until it became strong enough to become sin. Personally, I turned the other way. Nibbling usually is an innocent distant view of sin, but if the grass looks greener on the other side, Satan encourages us to nibble just a little. He probably would misquote the scripture, like he did with Jesus, and say, "Try me, test me, prove me, and see if I won't open the windows and let you have fun." He is a liar, and his ways never lead toward the abundant life.

Telling jokes is a way of nibbling in sin. I have been at many church parties where we shared jokes. Clean ones, of course! I don't remember ever getting past a few jokes until just a little "nibbling" started and implied dirt began to show up. God puts plenty of humor into conversations if they are about him and Jesus. Frances and I never have a dull minute and laugh far more than jokes can bring about. We believe in having a good time, but we do it by *feasting* on the manna instead of *nibbling* in sin.

"Prove all things; hold fast that which is good. Abstain from all *appearance* of evil." (I Thes. 5:21-22 KJV)

I'm sure this "nibble" will speak to a very large number of "Christians": Getting too familiar on dates—letting our emotions overshadow the voice of the Holy Spirit. It's the "playing around" to get the feel of the situation when God is saying "don't touch" that leads beyond the nibbling line of no return. Nibbling seems justifiable if we are ever so lightly considering giving way to a temptation. The

91

gravity pull toward sin gets stronger and stronger as we weaken little by little—then all too suddenly sin comes in to destroy and kill. Among Christians engaged to be married, this can change a Godly beauty to an ugly adultery and a lifetime of guilt can result if we let emotions get out of control. God is gracious and marvelous to forgive us of our sins, but he doesn't forgive in advance the ones you are about to commit. That willful, deliberate sin of placing the god of sex over the Almighty God looks highly distorted when seen in the floodlight of God. It's not possible to compliment God and Jesus by preferring any other gods.

Peter, do you love me?

Peter, do you love me?

Peter, do you love me?

Or will we, too, deny him when the pleasures of this world are made available?

"Once you were alienated from God and were enemies in your minds because of your evil behavior. But now he has reconciled you by Christ's physical body through death to present you holy in his sight, without blemish and free from accusation—if you continue in your faith, established and firm, not moved from the hope held out in the gospel." (Col. 1:21-23 NIV)

"Submit yourselves therefore to God. Resist the devil, and he will flee from you." (James 4:7 KJV)

"For he chose us in him before the creation of the world to be holy and blameless in his sight." (Eph. 1:4 NIV)

Jesus said, "FOLLOW ME"

But he doesn't nibble in sin!

SHOOT
CUSSIN—;*!"%=!

Poppa was a sinner! Then he met Jesus in a very personal way when I was about eight years old, and the world around our house changed. He wasn't mean—he was a very wonderful father, even before he became a Christian.

One of Poppa's very most proficient sins was his special vocabulary of curse words. He must have really had a high degree (Cus.D. instead of PhD) from that school because I believe he could match the sum of all cursing experts. Maybe he used that vocabulary to make up for his lack of "nice" adjectives—he used them for exclamation points, conjunctions, prepositions, commas, periods, semi-colons, dashes, asterisks, and some special ones he invented!*;. Even attitudes could be expressed by his unauthorized grammar.

I always admired and respected Poppa. I suppose I was somewhat "awed" by him. He only whipped me twice and thumped my ears a few corrective times, all of which (in his opinion) I needed. Much later in life I agreed, but not at the time, probably. He was a severe disciplinarian. We kids knew our bounds and learned quickly that it was more pleasant to want to do things that pleased him. He was severe because he loved us!

"I continually discipline and punish everyone I love; so I must punish you, unless you turn from your indifference and become enthusiastic about the things of God." (Revelation 3:19)

Kids who love their parents try to be like them so they learn quickly to do everything they can like grown-ups. One day my sister Frances, just older than I, made me mad. In fact at least two times she did that. One time I hit her across the shins with a broom handle . . . just as I wrote that I remembered how just before it hit her I felt bad inside but the momentum was too strong to stop my swing. Ever since then it has hurt me that I would have done such a thing. The Holy Spirit convicted me of my wrong even as a small child. The other time I got mad at her I started cursing her. So far as I know, I had never used any curse words out loud in my life before that, but my father had taught me thoroughly "all" of his words and I used them all—several times each! When I realized what I had done, I was crushed inside and felt mean and dirty. That's probably why I never cursed again in my whole life. I just didn't want to and I knew that it was wrong before anyone ever told me.

After Poppa got saved Jesus cleaned up his mouth and habits. One time before he was saved Poppa went off into the woods for two days and nights without his pipe and tobacco to try to quit smoking, just for Mama. He discovered it just wouldn't work, so he smoked night and day until the Spirit of God spoke to him. Then without a trip to the woods he just quit smoking—for Jesus.

That really is how Jesus gives us power to rid us of bad habits—when we do it for him! Poppa quit cursing soon after he and Mama got saved.

One day Mama was watching Poppa take the rim off of a Model T Ford to repair a flat. The Ford Company hadn't engineered a way of repairing flats that would cooperate with you and it was easy to smash your fingers. Poppa was really struggling, and each time he would hurt his finger he would say "Aw, shoot!" After hearing him say this many times, Mama said, "Poppa, you haven't quit cussin', you just changed words! Now you're 'shoot cussin'."

I don't remember ever hearing him even "shoot-cuss" after that. So strong was the desire in my mother and father to do what God wanted them to that they disciplined themselves to move as far away from any form of ungodliness as they could. That's probably where I learned in my heart to move as far away from sin as I could. The Bible says to resist the devil and he will flee from you. It also says to draw close to God and he will draw close to you. (James 4, 7-8) That's also what I mean by not "nibbling" in sin.

During the past few years since I started wanting to please God instead of trying to please myself, he started revealing more and more of the dross in me. He began to apply the fire of his Spirit to remove impurities. (He still is doing this as little "Christian sins" come to the surface to be skimmed off like dross, as I allow him to do it.) Sins can only be "Christian" sins when the Christian wants to be separated from them. The

95

only time we sin is when we want to. I don't want to sin because that means I want my way instead of God's way. But God's smeltering process in purifying me has not been to burn me by applying too much heat at one time. He does little by little what he knows is best.

In my seeking his will for my life he began to point out little unsuspecting flecks of impurity in the form of "crutches" I used in talking. He began to show me scriptures, and then to show my impurities in relation to these scriptures. Let me show you how he talked to me.

Let's look at the scriptures first: Ephesians 4, starting at verse 17.

> [17,18] Let me say this, then, speaking for the Lord: Live no longer as the unsaved do, for they are blinded and confused. Their closed hearts are full of darkness; they are far away from the life of God because they have shut their minds against him, and they cannot understand his ways. [19] They don't care anymore about right and wrong and have given themselves over to impure ways. They stop at nothing, being driven by their evil minds and reckless lusts.
>
> [20] But that isn't the way Christ taught you! [21] If you have really heard his voice and learned from him the truths concerning himself, [22] then throw off your old evil nature—the old you that was a partner in your evil ways—rotten through and through, full of lust and sham.
>
> [23] Now your attitudes and thoughts must all be constantly changing for the

better. ²⁴ Yes, you must be a new and different person, holy and good. Clothe yourself with this new nature.

²⁵ Stop lying to each other; tell the truth, for we are parts of each other and when we lie to each other we are hurting ourselves. ²⁶ If you are angry, don't sin by nursing your grudge. Don't let the sun go down with you still angry—get over it quickly; ²⁷ for when you are angry you give a mighty foothold to the devil.

²⁸ If anyone is stealing he must stop it and begin using those hands of his for honest work so he can give to others in need. ²⁹ Don't use bad language. <u>Say only what is good and helpful to those you are talking to, and what will give them a blessing.</u>

"Keep away from every kind of evil" ("Abstain from all appearance of evil." KJV) (I Thes. 5:22)

"You shall not use the name of Jehovah your God irreverently, nor use it to swear to a falsehood. You will not escape punishment if you do." (Exodus 20:7)

Col. 3:

SINCE YOU BECAME alive again, so to speak, when Christ arose from the dead, now set your sights on the rich treasures and joys of heaven where he sits beside God in the place of honor and power. ² Let heaven fill your thoughts; don't spend your time worrying about things down here. ³ You should have as little desire for this world as a dead person does. Your real life is in heaven with

Christ and God. [4] And when Christ who is our real life comes back again, you will shine with him and share in all his glories.

[5] Away then with sinful, earthly things; deaden the evil desires lurking within you; have nothing to do with sexual sin, impurity, lust and shameful desires; don't worship the good things of life, for that is idolatry. [6] God's terrible anger is upon those who do such things. [7] You used to do them when your life was still part of this world; [8] but now is the time to cast off and throw away all these rotten garments of anger, hatred, cursing, and dirty language.

Matt. 5:

[33] "Again, the law of Moses says, 'You shall not break your vows to God, but must fulfill them all.' [34] But I say: Don't make any vows! And even to say, 'By heavens!' is a sacred vow to God, for the heavens are God's throne. [35] And if you say 'By the earth!' it is a sacred vow, for the earth is his footstool. And don't swear 'By Jerusalem!' for Jerusalem is the capital of the great King. [36] Don't even swear 'By my head!' for you can't turn one hair white or black. [37] Say just a simple 'Yes, I will' or 'No, I won't. Your word is enough. To strengthen your promise with a vow shows that something is wrong."

Matt. 12:

[33] "A tree is identified by its fruit. A tree from a select variety produces good fruit; poor varieties don't. [34] You brood

of snakes! How could evil men like you speak what is good and right? For a man's heart determines his speech. [35] A good man's speech reveals the rich treasures within him. An evil-hearted man is filled with venom, and his speech reveals it. [36] And I tell you this, that you must give account on Judgment Day for every idle word you speak. [37] Your words now reflect your fate then: either you will be justified by them or you will be condemned."

Matt. 5:

[21] "Under the laws of Moses the rule was, 'If you kill, you must die.' [22] But I have added to that rule,[c] and tell you that if you are only *angry*, even in your own home,[d] you are in danger of judgment! If you call your friend an idiot, you are in danger of being brought before the court. And if you curse him, you are in danger of the fires of hell.[c]

Now let's look at some of the common impurities which I'll describe as "shoot-cussin'." These are expressions learned from our former father, Satan, just as I learned them from my earthly father. We go talking along using our word crutches which begin to describe our inner attitudes until we become what we say (we are saying what we really are inside). We Christians are too "nice" and "righteous" to use profanity like sinners do, aren't we? Or, are we? Are we trying to see how close we can get to the alfalfa patch, or the Egypt of sin, and still reside in the abundance of Canaan; the abundance offered only in Holy living. The Bible says ". . . one who is not holy will not see the Lord." (Heb. 12:14)

People in crime often change their name and use as an alias names bearing the same initials. In Satan's pattern of counterfeiting God's ways, he also uses similar sounding expressions, or names bearing the same initials. Actually Christians counterfeit Satan's language.

Our attitudes are still the same as they were before Jesus made us new creatures—they just seem nicer!

Look at these "Shoot Cussin" expressions:

VULGAR PROFANITY
    Aw, shoot
    Shucks
    Bull
    Baloney
    Garbage
    Pshaw
    Aw, Pfftt!
    Shaft
    Darn it
    Dag-nab-it, dang it, or dad-gum it
    Son of a gun
    Raise Cain
    Heck
    What in the Sam Hill
    Teed off, ticked off
    Pain in the neck
    That's a lot of stuff
    Butter hit the fan
    A lot of Malarky

VAIN—PROFANE USE OF GOD'S OR JESUS' NAME
O my gosh
By golly
God
Jesus
Jesus Christ
Jeepers Creepers (JC)
Jimminy Crickets (JC)
Jumping Jehosephat
Good gracious
Good grief
Good Gosh

SWEAR BY (Matt. 5:33-37 quoted above):
I swear
I swear to God
My word

SUBSTITUTE GOOD FOR BAD — OPPOSITE
For heaven's sake
Oh, heavens
What on earth
What in the world?
What in heaven's name? (God or Jesus)
How in blazes

SELF ESTEEM — VAIN
Bless God
Bless Patty
Bless my soul
My goodness (our goodness is as filthy rags)
My gracious
My, oh my

My, my
Mercy
Mercy goodness

Then there are those expressions which are another form of substitution, shoot cussin', but are languages attributed to Satan and his kingdom:

"Luck"—Jesus is the answer, and we don't need luck. Read Matthew 6:25-34; Jesus says the heathen worry—we don't need to; we have a sure thing. We even had someone recently say "Good luck in your miracle service." Expressions like this are common: "Better luck next time; Good luck, Tough luck".

Fortunately
I'll bet you
Knock on wood
Black Cat
Cross your heart and hope to die
Walk under ladder
Cross your fingers
Throw salt over your shoulder
Thirteen (13)
Weird — mostly pertaining to ill fortune, omen,
    spell, charm, soothsayer, witchcraft.
By chance
("Did you by chance remember to go by the
    store for me?")

One day Joanie, our daughter, came home from college and attended our home church when we couldn't be there. Afterwards she was excitedly telling of a miracle of healing in the church service. She began her story by saying "it was really *weird* how the person got healed." I was shocked and said, "Joanie, don't you realize you are referring to the work of the Holy Spirit with a satanic term?" I didn't fully know the meaning of the word, but I knew of a TV show where they referred to weird—and it was really "weird". It was a horror sort of a witchcraft show, if I remember correctly. Anyway, I knew it wasn't right. Bless her submissive heart, she started reminding kids at school that you glorify Satan when you use his terms. I think she changed about half the students who had been using the word.

Other terms of this nature are:

Freaked out
Spookey
Dopey
Goofey
Gee Whiz
Scare the wits out of you

I remember how as an adult I used to love to watch a TV show that showed witchcraft in an unsuspecting fun way. Little did I realize that this was the early stages of a plan of Satan to bring witchcraft to an all time high in America. There are now thousands of "witches" working for Satan and I believe a lot of them got their ideas to go into this evil power from watching programs like the one I especially loved.

God has some very harsh things to say about any form of witchcraft:

"When thou art come into the land which the Lord thy God giveth thee, thou shalt not learn to do after the abominations of those nations.

"There shall not be found among you any one that maketh his son or his daughter to pass through the fire, or that useth divination, or an observer of times, or an enchanter, or a witch, or a charmer, or a consulter with familiar spirits, or a wizard, or a necromancer. For all that do these things are an abomination unto the Lord: and because of these abominations the Lord thy God doth drive them out from before thee. Thou shalt be perfect with the Lord thy God." (Deut. 18:9-12) (KJV)

"I will put an end to all witchcraft—there will be no more fortune tellers to consult—and destroy all your idols." (Micah 5:12)

"But when you follow your own wrong inclinations your lives will produce these evil results: impure thoughts, eagerness for lustful pleasure, idolatry, spiritism (that is, encouraging the activity of demons). . . ." (Galatians 5:19)

Refer again to Matt. 12:34-35 quoted above, and see how words and thoughts affect us and others: "You brood of snakes! How could evil men like you speak what is good and right? For a man's heart determines his speech. A good man's speech reveals the rich treasures within him. An evil-hearted man is filled with venom, and his speech reveals it."

Fear is one of the most horribly depressing agents of Satan's spirits in use today. We can ask people in an audience who are depressed or are under a cloud of fear to stand and we are amazed at the magnitude of his satanic control. Where do we get our early training? Look at some of these familiar "schools" where we educate our children:

"Don't do that or the boogie man will get you!"

"Boo!"

We teach them to be afraid of the dark by saying: "The goblins (or gremlins) will get you" or "A ghost will get you."

We encourage or allow them to watch scary TV programs.

We speak of policemen in a way to educate ourselves to fear them.

"Be nice or the good fairy won't visit you."

"Put the tooth that was pulled under your pillow so the good fairy will leave you a quarter."

We all receive early training and carefully pass on to our children phrases and "sayings", teaching them where their security is, and how to get their world in order "without giving the glory to God and to Jesus" (How very coy and canny is Satan in his counterfeiting deceit).

The first of these I remember is:

"Star light, star bright, the first star I've seen tonight.

I wish I may, I wish I might

Have the wish I wish tonight."

Wouldn't it be better to teach them that Jesus takes care of each day's problems (Col. 2:6). That you can actually talk to God and to Jesus and get answers, instead of placing your hopes on a wish or on a star.

A few months ago we were back stage in an auditorium before a miracle service began. A little boy three or four years old was trying to operate a candy machine and hurt his finger. He started crying and his mother, in baby talk, started saying: "Let mommie kiss it so it will stop hurting." Certainly a mother's love and kisses are blessed and soothing, and I praise God for the tenderness he instills in a loving mother. I was standing near enough to reach his hurt finger and as I touched it I softly said "In Jesus name, pain, I rebuke you." Instantly the pain was gone and he stopped crying. Think of the impact we can have by giving Jesus the opportunity to bless little children today just like he did 2,000 years ago. We can teach them to know Jesus is always available. I think it would be wonderful to kiss the hurt finger as we ask Jesus to be the answer to a child's problems.

"Hay, hay; make a wish and turn away."

"Honk as you drive through an underpass — for luck."

Another very powerful tool of Satan to establish his negative ways within us, usually at an early age, are unendearing, suppressing terms such as:

Dumb-bell
Dum-dum
Dummy
Dodo (A flightless, clumsy bird)
Stupid
Stupid Jerk
Crazy
Silly

Ignoramus

Lame-brain

Bird brain

Flea brain

* Idiot

* Fool

* Shame on you (an innocent sounding attempt to place a curse on someone.)

* (See Matt. 5:21-22 quoted above.)

We found a real live example of the effect of these terms in our own home and hopefully we have just about overcome it. Our Joanie has a big brother, Tom. Tom constantly substituted names when speaking to Joanie like "stupid," "dum-dum" "jocko" "yo yo," all words to suppress mentally.

Joanie first came into my life as my daughter at age sixteen and I noticed she always felt inferior in intelligence. She would make remarks like "I'm just not smart enough to learn that; I'm just not going to be able to pass that subject; I don't think I could ever make it through college." I learned very soon that Joanie had one of the sharpest, practical and intelligent minds I had known. I realized that the innocent-sounding terms, coupled with the exceedingly high IQ of Tom, had so suppressed Joanie's opinion of her own intellect that she was being pushed into an imaginary corner of inadequacy and actually becoming what she had been "innocently" called. Frances and I began encouraging her and assuring her of her "brain capacity" and diverting references to a negative power. Satan is always negative; Jesus is always positive. Satan makes the negative appear positive. I heard her one day answer the phone "this is dum-dum." Quickly I asked her to correct any reference by her friends to such names. I told her to have them call her "smart-smart." More recently when Tom's son David was learning to talk, Tom had him referring to himself as "dumb-alligator." We told him about our long and difficult struggle to overcome the negative effect this had cn Joanie. The next time we heard from little David he was calling himself "smart alligator!"

Frances and I were having dinner with Joan and Bob (her husband), and Bob's sister Martha the night after I began writing this chapter. I began making notes as they talked at the dinner table, extracting "shoot-cussin' " or other phrases from their conversation. Bob almost quit talking as I jotted down "lucky", "fortunately" and a few other such terms. Then Frances said "Did you by any chance call about...." Much "corrective" laughter followed as I made a note, because one of Frances' favorite scriptures is "And we know that all things work together for good to them that love God, to them who are called according to his purpose." (Romans 8:28) (KJV) God doesn't do things by chance. Martha remained somewhat quiet through all this until I remarked that she hadn't said much. She replied, "I'm *afraid* to speak for *fear* I'll *shoot-cuss*!"

I believe that if we use these pseudo-Christian terms and phrases, we give glory to Satan and encourage within ourselves and others the activities of spirits. We make it seem "all right" or "normal" to play around with Satan's tools. We might try to call this a "white" abomination unto God like we attempt to make a misleading statement, or slight lie sacred by tagging it with a "sanctified" label of a "white lie." If we need to add to our speech, why not add words and phrases to exalt Jesus and to give praise and glory to God—where all praise and all glory and all honor belong. I don't hesitate to express to my CPA clients terms I say because they are in my heart, such as:

Hallelujah
Praise the Lord
Praise Jesus
Amen
Glory
Thank you, Jesus
And our own special ones. . . .
    Hang Loose with Jesus
    God is Fabulous!

I commented to an attorney client about this "shoot-cussin' " chapter one day by saying I was going to put some of his terms in the book. Just a few days ago as I left his office he included "Hallelujah!" in his parting comment. I turned quickly back and told him I would put him in the book again! He said, "But that isn't regular." I replied "It can be!"

"Remember what Christ taught and let his

words enrich your lives and make you wise; teach them to each other and sing them out in psalms and hymns and spiritual songs, singing to the Lord with thankful hearts. And whatever you do or say, let it be as a representative of the Lord Jesus, and come with him into the presence of God the Father to give him your thanks." (Colossians 4:16-17)

GLORY, HALLELUJAH!!!

LITTLE BITTY Charles

God is relentless in his transforming power when we "want" to follow his laws and honestly seek his way for our lives.

Frances and I casually discussed sometime during the few days we were together just before we were married, a subject which seemingly had little significance but which became one of the most difficult problems of my life. Even now it's hard to call it by its true name—"EGO", the "I" or self of a person, especially when that person is "me." And even more especially when "I" want to be captain of my soul instead of letting Jesus be king of my life. Come to think of it, Satan became who he is for the same reason! He lost! I want to win my battle. Satan was thrown out of heaven like a bolt of lightning because of his ego. I prefer to be rocketed into heaven because of Jesus!

Neatly tucked under the glass top of my desk in my home study (by my Frances), right where I see it every time I sit at my desk, is a printed invitation which reads:

You are invited to meet and hear

Frances Gardner Hunter

(and Charles too!)

SATURDAY EVENING - NOVEMBER 18, 1972
Banquet Room of Holiday Inn North at 1-30

PRAYER HOUR begins at 5 P.M.
Buffet ($2.95) in Restaurant at 6:16 P.M.
(Songs by Young People during Buffet)

Old Fashioned SONG SERVICE - Banquet Room at 7:15

FELLOWSHIP and SPEAKERS at 8 P.M.
Come to all or any part as Christ leads.

Frances lovingly helps me face this situation honestly by indicating with a "little bitty" space between her thumb and forefinger "little bitty Charles." We had made all arrangements for speakers as a *team,* all our letters clearly indicated this. Our correspondence highlighted it, our stationery showed it, our publicity pictures and news release proclaimed it, our telephone calls with the director of the meeting and his reply pointed it out—in fact, everything looked just right about our reception as a "team" and it made me feel *real good* inside until—at the last minute I saw the little bitty "and Charles too!" tickets, I was crushed! For a while my insides felt like everyone in the world had seen this invitation. God wanted me to see not just "little bitty Charles," but he knew "self" must be dead before Jesus could have full control. Self can never be made small enough for Jesus to live with—it must be removed to make room for him only.

God told Ezekiel: "There is special meaning in each detail of what I have told you to do...." (Ezekiel 4:3) Then God told him to lie on his left side for 390 days and on his right side for 40 days, demonstrating a point he wanted to make to the

112

Israelites. In my search for God's control over my life, I didn't have to go through 430 days like Ezekiel did; God dealt with me for three years and taught me that "there is special meaning in each detail of what he told me to do"—including "little bitty Charles!"

During the first wonderful year of my new life when I was meditating so constantly in the Bible certain scriptures were brightly focused into my mind by the Holy Spirit. I could not understand at the time why God so strongly stressed them, yet I knew he was drawing my attention to them for a purpose. I would read, ask God their deep meaning and go back to them again and again and still not find their meaning in my life. This points out a tremendous meaning of the verse "Thy Word have I hid in my heart, that I might not sin against thee." (Psalm 119:11 KJV). I didn't try to memorize those "focused" verses but God "hid" them in my heart-mind for the time he would recall them for my understanding. One such verse was "He who is greatest among you shall be your servant; whoever exalts himself will be humbled, and whoever humbles himself will be exalted." (Matt. 23:11-12 RSV). Little did I realize how I would need to be reminded of this but God knew how he would have to break me all the way.

I sincerely felt I had given all to Jesus because I so wanted to be his disciple. I thought humility was one of my greatest traits (I was probably a little proud of being so humble). I tried to demonstrate being humble to my partners and staff, to my clients and their employees and to my wife. I was really willing to be a servant for Jesus!

Then God changed the whole course of my life!

A minister brought me a little book to read which he felt would bring cheer into what many thought was a dark period in my life. Actually, it was the sunrise of my life and in it was no darkness. This little book was called "God Is Fabulous" by a Miami businesswoman. I laughed and cried my way through it. Here was another person who had discovered the same miraculous life I had found. I knew someday I would meet that person. God had introduced me to my beloved Frances through her book, even before he told me anything of his plans.

Then he introduced us in person! As we approached the date of our marriage we made a famous "innocent, insignificant" (so I thought) decision: Frances had three best selling books all bearing the author's name "Frances Gardner." Our discussion concluded (humbly) that she would continue to write and speak under the pen name "Frances Gardner" since she was already known by that name. We agreed that this would leave our private lives free of the public influence so we could be just what we wanted, "Mr. and Mrs. Charles Hunter." Frances said "Charles, you are going to face many problems about this. Your ego will bother you when you are not recognized as my husband." I assured her there could not possibly be any problem because when you are fully yielded to God, "self" must always be dead. Besides, the Bible said if you want to be great, you must be humble.

We were married a day or two later, moved to Houston and began our life as Mr. and Mrs. Charles Hunter. It was so beautiful and peaceful and my only longing was that God would let us be together more. She was away from home over half the time the first six months of our marriage.

I suppose about six weeks had passed and Frances was in the Eastern part of the United States and I had gone to Corpus Christi, Texas to see my parents for one day (my Dad was critically ill). I anxiously returned home because I knew I would have a letter waiting for me because Frances always wrote and called every day. As soon as I got home, my heart thrilled as I tore open the letter from my Sweetheart. Love just gushed from the paper and my heart was light and full of her love and the love of God and Christ Jesus she shared with me. Then I looked at some enclosures, newspaper clippings, bulletins, announcements, etc. One clipping was a front-page article and picture of my own sweet wife. Under the picture was the caption "Frances Gardner speaks." It was like a bolt of lightning struck dead center in my heart. The light I had felt as I read the letter suddenly turned to darkness. For about thirty minutes I couldn't shake the feeling. I began to cry with loneliness and grief. A deep depression came over me. I don't believe I ever felt worse. I rushed to our bedroom, fell on my knees and cried out to God "If this is Satan, get him out of here, and Father, draw near to me!" Instantly a beautiful peace flooded my soul and it was like depression and darkness had suddenly been sucked away by a giant vacuum cleaner and light flooded into my heart and soul! What a difference! How very important it is for the Holy Spirit to put the Word of God in the storehouse of our hearts—I had read and meditated hundreds of hours and in my time of need the meaning of two verses were recalled by the Holy Spirit, and I was delivered! "Submit yourselves therefore to God. Resist the devil and he will flee from you. Draw near to God and he will draw near to you." (James 4:7-8) (RSV).

Just now as I referred back to the Bible to copy the above scripture, the meaning of which I had hidden in my heart, I looked at verse 6, just above it: "But he gives more grace; therefore it says, *God opposes the proud, but gives grace to the humble.'* " God is relentless, isn't he?

I thought that problem of the name "Gardner" was short-lived, and I was glad. But still it was in my mind. God had so quickly come to my rescue that his love and presence overshadowed the realization that I didn't want to be married to Frances "Gardner"—I wanted her to be Frances Hunter all the time.

That night Frances called and before I told her anything of my adventure, she said that afternoon she realized she wanted nothing more than to be the wife of Charles Hunter. She said she didn't want to be Frances Gardner, she wasn't Frances Gardner and she wanted to immediately make such changes as were needed to put this into effect. God had spoken to both of us in different ways by saying exactly the same thing to each, even though we were more than a thousand miles apart physically, yet one in Jesus and one in marriage.

Closely connected with this intense desire to have Frances as my very own, came another attack by Satan. I love the way God takes all the battles the devil starts and maneuvers them into a victory to carry out his strategy for our life.

We had been married less than two months when Frances started on a thirty-three day tour of the central and western part of the United States. She had booked this tour long before. We were so completely sure that God was in charge of our lives that no matter what he wanted us to do, we were willing to do it, even if it meant being apart.

Joan and I accompanied Frances for the first three days on a week-end. I can assure you the fiery darts of the wicked are genuine and can penetrate your very heart except for the shield of protection God always has around his children. As we entered the front of the church where Frances was speaker, she was greeted exuberantly—"Praise the Lord, Mrs. Gardner, we're thrilled to have you" and away they whisked her, leaving Joanie and me standing alone. I felt totally abandoned by Frances, ignored by "her" public, and separated from being any part of her or her ministry.

I was taken to a Sunday School class later that morning where I shared how God had transformed my life as I met Jesus in a personal way. Yet, inside I was lonely and my attitude wasn't the most loving toward those who took her from me. Loneliness is actually what we find when we take our eyes off Jesus and look at ourselves; that is never a scenic view. Then came the intermission between services and I was back with Frances for a few minutes and I felt I could never stand being separated again. But here came the pastor and said "come on Frances, let's go to the front"—and he (the minister—I saw him as a monster) fled away with my bride, and again I was alone.

That afternoon Joan and I had to leave Frances for that long thirty more days—and nights, which were worse than the days if that was possible. Never have I had my heart torn so much as when we parted. I could see for the first time it had the same effect on her. We both cried in the arms of each other.

The next day Frances called and sounded excited as she told of the miracles of changed lives and then told of a wealthy Christian (I had met him that week-end) taking her through a huge, luxurious apartment project God had given him, and how God had so beautifully provided that he would fly her in his private twin engine plane a few hundred miles away to her next engagement. After the call, there came a barrage of fiery darts and I could hardly stand the thought of someone else being with her so much when I was not there. A million thoughts (darts) shot at my mind-heart and I was miserable and growing worse as the night hours slowly moved along while I waited for her late night call. I felt a jealousy flaring up in my inner being. I reasoned that it was not a jealousy of the preacher, or the businessman, but just a jealousy of those people who had her when I didn't. One thing I knew without a doubt—there was no question of her loyalty and faithfulness to me, yet she was there and I was a thousand miles away—alone. I decided I couldn't add to her long hours by telling her of my struggle. Besides, I couldn't tell her there was jealousy in me!

Then the phone rang and we had hardly said we loved each other before I knew to be totally honest I must tell her my innermost thoughts and attitudes. I opened my heart to her as tears burst from my eyes and my voice, and as soon as I finished, and admitted there was some kind of jealousy in me, she immediately said "I know, honey. I already knew before you called." I know her heart was torn more than mine. She just began to pray to God the most heart-felt outpouring cry to him I've ever heard, and so full of love. I wish I had the full prayer to share with you. Since it was not recorded, let me share the letter I wrote her the next morning:

5:45 A.M.
2-25 of Fabulous 1970

Good Morning My Heavenly Wife,
My Sweetheart,

Last nite after midnite I was a part of the most beautiful love miracle God ever poured out on any human! Thank God that the jealous nature in me stuck its head out because of my exclusive devotion to you, just long enough for God to absorb it through you, then through Christ and into God himself as it was washed away in the most beautiful prayer of love ever

119

uttered from the very heart of a woman. Never before has a man been so wonderfully blessed as God has blessed me. When love comes so totally from your heart which was made to love me by the very act of God as he gave you to me on October 3, 1969 when his Holy Spirit, your holy spirit and my spirit made holy by his love blended so purely; that love has been so refined and purified and filtered that it is genuinely holy love and no greater love has ever existed. That is the reason I sobbed last nite and again as I write this this morning as God bathes my soul to purify and cleanse my heart of the sin of jealousness because I asked him to cleanse it. Through your prayer last nite it was so miraculously removed. I pray that it will never again exist in me—certainly it has no cause to exist and that was made even plainer by your expression of a great and wonderful love last nite. Had you been physically in my arms where I want so much for you to be, you could not have been so close to me because I felt your spirit and mine were one, present in me. This is actually so because Christ said as the Father is in me, I am in you; and in John 15:3-4 (which I read to Joan last nite and which God's Holy Spirit opened the Bible to just now) "You are already made clean by the word which I have spoken to you. Abide in me and I in you." Sweetheart, you know how aware I am of the assured fact that my love for you and yours for me was and is from the beginning wholly of God and that I have absolutely no doubt of this. There has never existed any cause for me to doubt the completeness of your love for me, and so even as the devil stepped in last nite (and actually he has used this same attack before) I had no reason to doubt your complete love, faithfulness and loyalty to me; but I'm glad God, as he so often does, used the devil to bring out a sin, so that he could reveal himself to me in yet another way. I love him and you, and I guess because he ordained your love for me, this love is one and the same. I had never before heard the exclusiveness of love of a woman for her one man expressed so vividly as when you said in your prayer (really a prayer through Christ and God to me) that all other men are nothing but flesh to you. Baby, you can be absolutely sure that this is so in my love for you—I love you so very, very deeply, and you know how that love began as I prayed to God that if he wanted me to love you, he would cause me to fall deeply in love with you, beyond any love I could imagine or know; then how for three days I physically felt this love start flowing through my veins till I was so soon, deeply in love with you; my love continues to grow deeper and deeper till I cannot imagine its depth and yet it continues to grow. What a magnificent God we serve and how true he spoke when he said if we would bring ourselves 100% to him (full tithes into the storehouse), put him to the test, he would open the windows of heaven for us and pour down for us an overflowing blessing. And then to show how he will purify a sin of jealousy he continued in Malachi 3:11 to say "I will rebuke the devourer for you, so that it will not destroy the fruits of your soil; and your vine in the field shall not fail to bear." Eve and Adam let the devourer destroy their fruit, but through our Lord Jesus Christ whom we both love so much, our love will always flourish in our garden of God's love made by God just for our own and for both of us together. I love you with all my heart, mind, soul, and body!

Your Charles

Frances felt the impact of this struggle within me and knew at the heart of it all was the "self" of the man she loved. She wanted so much to be the submissive wife to the husband who wanted to be her husband and to be the head of the house, privileged to love her and protect her. But more than our burning love for each other was our constraining love of God, and we both knew we must in all things put God first. Neither of us would have considered her withdrawing from the life God gave her to share with a world so in need of knowing an exciting, living Jesus. She saw clearly that at every turn the name Gardner was flounced in my face, ever reminding me that we were separated by a name and yet one in flesh.

I began crying to God to take away all of my resistance to that name. I said "no matter what you have to do to rid me of my attitude about it, get it out of my life forever. If I'm not getting into the Bible enough, keep me awake all night if you have to, but clear this out of my life. Just give me enough sleep to keep me going." That night I woke up about two o'clock and got right out of bed and read the Bible for almost two hours. It was in the Old Testament and was exactly what I needed as the Spirit of God ministered to my need. The next night was a repeat, but as I began reading where I stopped the night before, I almost went to sleep and it was just a series of meaningless words. I said "God, that isn't where you want me to read." Immediately I turned to the first chapter of James and I knew God had said exactly where. Listen to what he spoke in my testing period: *"Charles* (not Dear Brothers), is your life full of difficulties and temptations? *(I said, "God you know it!")* Then be happy, *(I want to, God)* for when the way is rough, *(Has it ever been rough this week, Father!)* your patience has a chance to grow. (OK, Father, do anything, but get my attitude about 'Gardner' healed). So let it grow, and don't try to squirm out of your problems. For when your patience is finally in full bloom, then you will be ready for anything, strong in character, full and complete." (OK, Father, I'll just turn loose, and be patient and what does it really matter what they call Frances, because I know you will do whatever is needed). I had lost seven pounds in seven days and nights of struggle. If we could just realize that the battle is the Lord's. He will give us rest and peace if we will cease being self, and just be the temple where Jesus can live and do his work in us and through us—"it is not I who live, but Christ who lives within me."

Charles, TURN LOOSE!

God provided unexpectedly that I could go to California in the middle of the thirty days. The beginning of the nine days we were to be together was at Campus Crusade for Christ headquarters in Arrowhead Springs. We met the man in charge of a seminar being conducted during the day (not the one in which we were speakers). He had never heard of Frances and this was nice because she was introduced as Mrs. Hunter, my wife. He discovered from someone there that she had written several books and was a speaker. He wanted to take us to four different groups in study sessions to introduce us. In the first room he said "This is Frances Hunter and her husband, uh-uh-uh-ah. . . ." He was embarrassed that he had forgotten my name. In the next room he had full confidence, so he introduced us "This is Frances Gardner and her husband Charles Hunter." I said "Thank you, Father—see it isn't bothering me at all." I even pleasantly laughed about it. In the third room he said "This is Charles Gardner and his wife Frances." Again—peace! Victory! Frances was about to crawl under the floor because I hadn't had a chance to share with her this new found peace. I have forgotten the fourth introduction, but it was worse than ever. I thanked God and knew it was well worth the seven lost pounds to be rid of this "Gardner" problem once and for all.

We finally had Frances' books changed to show 'Frances Gardner Hunter' and I felt this would surely cause people to accept our marriage as genuine. But do you know what—people who had just read her first book and who looked at Frances Gardner Hunter would still call her Mrs. Gardner. We would be introduced constantly as Frances Gardner and her husband Charles Hunter. You are right—where did that peace and victory go? I would quickly (and sometimes curtly) correct them. One night a pastor introduced us as Frances Gardner and her husband Charles Hunter and I corrected him in front of his church, laughing and teasing him. He was so disturbed that at the end of the service he carefully stressed his thanks to Frances *HUNTER* and Charles "Gardner!!!" I rushed up to him because of the sudden flush in his face as he realized what he said, shook his hand in front of the laughing congregation and tried to dispel his frustration.

The more I have tried to correct the problem, the more it is aggravated. That's exactly what happens when we earnestly, sincerely ask God to solve a problem and instead of leaving it in his hands, we take it back and try to do it our way. God is real, you know (Charles) and he is quite capable of controlling people's minds. He can change any situation existing so easily, and wants to. He wants much more to deal with us until we trust his reality. Why can't we "turn loose" of our problems and let him do it his way? Why do we keep holding on to self when we know we must turn loose?

We have often recalled what I had once written in a letter to Frances before we were married: "I'll be happy if God just calls me to do nothing but carry your books." Be careful what you say to God—he hears everything!

125

You would think I would just give this problem to God and trust him to do the physical acts necessary to clear it out of my life. I had searched my heart and wanted to release it, but someway it has come back again and again. The world has been amused and blessed by the garbage problem in Keith Miller's life (Taste of New Wine). I don't know which is harder to dispose of—garbage or "Gardner." Really he had the same problem—it was not taking out the garbage—it was getting the garbage of self taken out of him.

God uses all kinds of ways to make us totally submissive to him. I thank and praise him for relentlessly dealing with me. Frances has said if God had told her everything wrong with her the day she accepted Jesus, she would have had a heart attack, or run in the opposite direction. I feel like God has won the Gardner battle at least 99.44% in my life. (God, hurry and get that last fraction of my holding on—I should say Charles, hurry and turn loose and don't grab it back). The last struggle I had, and it was a small one, came a few months ago and I laughed out loud right in the middle of my morning Bible reading. I can't recall what it was (probably 'little *biggy* Charles') but I was really trying to find 100% peace about it and again had asked God to help. He did!

I was meditating in the beautiful book of John that morning, just drinking in the last instructions, promises and assurances Jesus was giving his disciples before going back to heaven. Then came the fifteenth chapter: Jesus said, "I am the true Vine, and my Father is the *GARDNER.*" There

126

was a release within me as I said "God, you are my Father, and if you are a 'gardner,' that even makes me a 'gardner.'! Thank you, Father."

It wasn't long after that till I opened a letter addressed to Mr. and Mrs. Charles E. Hunter. In it was a small check made payable to Charles and Frances Gardner! It surprised me, but praise God, it didn't bother me.

Frances has been so very loving and patient and wise through this battle which could have been won very quickly and easily if I had "trusted" God completely. But what multitudes of blessings and growth I have received as God has taught me how to TURN LOOSE of self. Is it worth the effort to die to self as God confronts us with those inner attitudes of our heart to make us what he wants us to be? Let Jesus answer that question: "And Jesus replied, 'Let me assure you that no one has ever given up anything—home, brother, sisters, mother, father, children, or property (and he could add "self")—for love of me and to tell others the Good News, who won't be given back, a hundred times over, homes, brothers, sisters, mothers, children, and land—with persecutions! All these will be his here on earth, and in the world to come he shall have eternal life.' " (Mark 10:29-30)

Whoops! There he did it again—I just read the next verse (31) "But many people who seem to be *important* (there's that ego again) now will be the least important then; and many who are considered least here shall be greatest there." God, I accept being "little bitty Charles (even Charles Gardner if people call me that)—for your glory and the glory of Jesus. I love you, Jesus!"

As we counsel with and observe Christians, we notice many people who have the same "ego-self" problem. They are just scratching their way up a tree. That's what happened to Eve. She wanted what "she" wanted (self) and not what God wanted, and scratched up the *"Tree* of Conscience, giving knowledge of Good and Bad" when God had provided abundance of the best of fruit on the *"Tree* of Life" which is Jesus! (Gen. 2:8-10)

We get buried so deep in self that it takes a careful digging to reveal our living "self." When we are honest with ourselves, the Holy Spirit will clearly reveal what we are holding. When we ask God to do the miracle of crucifying self, we must do like Jesus did. God provided the plan for Jesus' death on the cross, but Jesus was the one who "volunteered" to be crucified. We must be crucified with Christ, and we must volunteer our self-death before Jesus can freely live his life in us and through us. Remember, it is not I who live, but Christ who lives within me. The longest trip we can take is from ourselves to Jesus, but Jesus said we must take the scenic route—the narrow way—the Highway of Holiness.

Luke 14:26-27 tells again "Anyone who wants to be my follower must love me far more than he does his own father, mother, wife, children, brothers, or sisters—yes, *more than his own life— otherwise he cannot be my disciple."*

Have I learned anything from "LITTLE BITTY Charles?"

Yes!

EGO HAS TO GO!!!!!

AND GOD SAID UNTO ME . . .

I dedicate this chapter particularly to those business men and women, but not to the exclusion of everyone else, who are willing to relinquish the management of their particular business or job to Jesus—the same Jesus to whom God relinquished the management of the earth, the universe, heaven, and in fact everything that was, and is, and is to come, everywhere. Can we trust Him?

Luke 10:
> [21] Then he was filled with the joy of the Holy Spirit and said, "I praise you, O Father, Lord of heaven and earth, for hiding these things from the intellectuals and worldly wise and for <u>revealing them to those who are as trusting as little children.</u>[c] <u>Yes, thank you, Father, for that is the way you wanted it.</u> [22] <u>I am the Agent of my Father in everything</u>; and no one really knows the Son except the Father, and no one really knows the Father except the Son and those to whom the Son chooses to reveal him."

We hear much about prayer—how to talk to God, but we need to find that sure way of hearing

God when he speaks to us. I believe God hears every thought and every uttered prayer. He hears when we don't even think we are praying, as well as when we know we are.

How he answers, when he answers, where he answers, how much he answers ... how can we business people, or we mothers with children, or husbands and wives, or children and parents, how can we reach heaven with prayers and hear God when he answers?

God spoke to prophets. Look at Daniel 10:7-14:

> 7 I, Daniel, alone saw this great vision; the men with me saw nothing, but they were suddenly filled with unreasoning terror and ran to hide, 8 and I was left alone. When I saw this frightening vision my strength left me, and I grew pale and weak with fright.
>
> 9 Then he spoke to me, and I fell to the ground face downward in a deep faint. 10 But a hand touched me and lifted me, still trembling, to my hands and knees. 11 And I heard his voice—"O Daniel, greatly beloved of God," he said, "stand up and listen carefully to what I have to say to you, for God has sent me to you." So I stood up, still trembling with fear.
>
> 12 Then he said, "Don't be frightened, Daniel, for your request has been heard in heaven and was answered the very first day you began to fast before the Lord and pray for understanding; that very day I was sent here to meet you. 13 But for twenty-one days the mighty Evil Spirit

who overrules the kingdom of Persia[a] blocked my way. Then Michael, one of the top officers of the heavenly army, came to help me, so that I was able to break through these spirit rulers of Persia. [14] Now I am here to tell you what will happen to your people, the Jews, at the end times—for the fullfillment of this prophecy is many years away."

First of all we must *want* to hear what *he wants* us to do. When we are working for Jesus, instead of our all-too-usual way of feeling he is working for us, then we take a different approach to reach heaven in prayer. Before I gave everything to God, it was difficult to give 13% of my income to him. Now that he has it all, I have no struggle—I just ask him how he wants me to manage *his* money. When I hear Frances' testimony I rarely hear one part without feeling God's Presence powerfully. She learned from the Holy Spirit the same thing God had used with such an impact to turn my life around. She had prayed—"God, don't let it hurt when they operate on my eye." Then a short time later (I'm sure the Holy Spirit put these words in her heart and mind) she held up her open hand to God and said, "God, give me back that prayer. When I get out of this hospital I'll spend the rest of my life seeing *what I can do for you, and not what you can do for me."* As a non-Christian she had said the secret of the Christian life. And she meant it! Twelve hundred miles away and three years later, a stranger to her, but not to God, I learned the same principle that God has shown her. Meditate on this principle until you reach the very foundation of its full meaning. This reverses our entire prayer communication.

Man's Communication Lost

When God created the earth, he was pleased.
When God created birds, fish and animals, he was pleased.
When God made man and maid, he was pleased.
These were all made in utter perfection.

God and man walked in perfect harmony on his perfect earth, and they talked to each other in perfect holy communication. Nothing needed to be changed—ever!

But sin of man made a perfect environment between a perfect God and a once perfect man, imperfect, and the "better than telephone wires" between heaven and earth were broken. But Jesus established a new creation, a new kingdom of heaven on earth! He gave us instant two way communication with God. It's through Jesus, and by using his Name, that we can go into the very presence of God and have personal talks with him—and he with us.

Men and women are now brought into existence through the reproductive design God used from the very beginning. Life came to man when God breathed into his nostrils the breath of life;—and man became a living soul, or living being.

We know that this human body and mind is the most fantastic functioning "thing" known to mankind. No rocket, no machine, no bomb, no electronic instrument, no computer can ever measure up to the God-created man. No wonder God was pleased. Into this self-contained man-unit, God put the "brain," its central control system. Scientists and physicians cannot fathom its expanse nor its capabilities, nor match its speed or accuracy. It is a two-way communication system intricately connected to every part of the body, to every tiny cell of the body and is in absolute control of everything inside the body in its healthy state. In a micro-instant of time a complete two-way "conversation" takes place between a toe someone just stepped on and the brain control when the toe screams to its master "help, I'm hurt!"

Right back from central comes the answer— "Yes, I know"; and micro-simultaneously the brain tells the hands and fingers to get down there quick and get the other guy's foot off yours. At the same time your brain tells your back to start bending, and your eyes to watch where you are going. It tells your radar senses to watch that your head doesn't hit the chair arm on the way down. Simultaneously it tells the mouth to say, "ooooooo" or if your mind is correctly on Jesus to send up to God that "ask and you shall receive" signal by announcing, "Jesus, do something!" Other parts of your mind are observing the size of the foot on yours, whether it's there intentionally or by accident and no telling what else is going on in this totally coordinated creation, even to the resurrection of attitudes and of events of the past!

If I crooked my finger at you, it would really not be my finger making that gesture. My brain directs every action of every part of my physical being. If my body functions normally, each part obeys my mind without questioning. They were created to carry out the orders of my brain. They are there to serve me and each other. They are servants, just as in Jesus' day wealthy men owned other people as slaves. The slaves were theirs and had to obey their every wish and command. Jesus was one such slave. He was owned and controlled by his Father God. He carried out in intricate detail every single instruction God gave him. He was a good servant and wanted to serve his Master. Jesus chose certain people to serve him while he was on earth. What a high honor that was. Then he made those same servants his friends. The brain is in control of all to which it is master every second of man's physical life.

And still deeper inside even than the brain, and more powerful, and more completely the master of this created "tent" is the real, everlasting man—the spirit. This spirit, superior to all else of this created being, is controlled by its master. In healthy state, this spirit is controlled by the Holy Spirit—God's Spirit. So beautiful and perfect is God's "man" that when properly submitted to the total control of God, his Holy Spirit is merged into man's spirit to become one. And there God dwells, in residence, in our spirit, living within our body. We are the temple of God. "For in Christ there is all of God in a human body; so you have everything when you have Christ, and you are filled with God through your union with Christ. He is the highest Ruler, with authority over every other power." (Col. 2:9-10)

"My prayer for all of them is that they will be of one heart and mind, just as you and I are, Father—that just as you are in me, and I am in you, so they will be in us, and the world will believe you sent me. . . ." "I have given them the glory you gave me—the glorious unity of being one, as we are—I in them and you in me, all being perfected into one—so that the world will know you sent me and will understand that you love them as much as you love me—these you've given me—so that they can see my glory. You gave me the glory because you loved me before the world began." (John 17:21-24)

The human mind wants to please the human body and give to it its desires. The spirit has a God-installed gyroscope which causes it to seek God and to please him.

Our human minds were given a free will or choice to please our spirit's master—God or Satan. We must choose one or the other—there is no third choice. If there was a third choice, we could choose to make ourselves master. When we want to please self, we are pleasing Satan. When we want to please God, we must deny ourselves. Jesus said: "If anyone wants to be a follower of mine, let him deny himself and take up his cross and follow me." (Matt. 16:24)

Galatians 5:16-18:
[16] I advise you to obey only the Holy

135

Spirit's instructions. He will tell you where to go and what to do, and then you won't always be doing the wrong things your evil nature wants you to. [17] For we naturally love to do evil things that are just the opposite from the things that the Holy Spirit tells us to do; and the good things we want to do when the Spirit has his way with us are just the opposite of our natural desires. <u>These two forces within us are constantly fighting each other to win control over us, and our wishes are never free from their pressures.</u> [18] When you are guided by the Holy Spirit you need no longer force yourself to obey Jewish laws.

All my life I could picture God speaking audibly to Moses, Elijah, Noah and the others in the Bible. Never once did I think he might have spoken "thought" messages—voiceless messages into their minds. Now it seems reasonable to me that when God told Abraham to start toward a land, the location of which he didn't know, for a purpose he hadn't been told fully, it would not have taken faith if God had sat down on a log with him and audibly spoken to him. I believe the Holy Spirit spoke to him exactly as he does to us today.

It takes faith to know you hear him and a very receptive mind and spirit to actually hear. Faith becomes substance when acted upon, without knowing, but simply trusting. I learn to trust more by acting upon the faith I have—whether large or small. If I miss, I don't let it embarrass me—if I hit and a miracle occurs, I praise God and tell others what he has done. If I don't act, nothing happens. We have a protective shield around us: "The steps of good men are directed by the Lord. He delights in each step they take. If they fall it isn't fatal, for the Lord holds them with his hand." (Psalms 37:23)

God would rather have us *listen to him* for instructions than to double our church giving. "Obedience is far better than sacrifice. He is much more interested in your listening to him than in your offering the fat of rams to him." (I Sam. 15:22)

If we want to hear God (and he does want us to hear him) it is quite a normal way of God-life to have him guide us in decisions.

If I am supervising men of my staff, I tell them what I want done, to some degree how to do it; then I review their work. I don't do it all for them—remember they work for me. The same is true with Jesus—he "supervises" our work and guides us. If my employee can't make a decision because of his lesser knowledge, or his lesser experience in making decisions, I either help him, or make the decision myself. We can go to Jesus, our supervisor, *for* a decision, or *for help* in making decisions.

These decisions must always be made or placed into our human mind—our brain. As we accumulate knowledge of our chosen profession or field of work, we store that into our brain for future use. The more information stored in the mind, the more facts we can apply in making a decision. We must not only store them in our memory bank, but we must be able to sort the facts, select the right ones, apply them to the circumstance of the moment, then make a judgement. This can all be accomplished by our mind.

If I need to know what 2 plus 2 equals, my mind simply recalls a formula or a memorized fact and I know the answer. This is done by thinking. God has the ability to place thoughts into the human mind, and so does Satan. We need to be able to distinguish our thoughts, God's thoughts and Satan's thoughts. In I Cor. 2:1-16, look at the ways Paul explains about the Holy Spirit speaking—I'll underline them for you. Look for ways you can know he speaks to you:

I CORINTHIANS:

2 DEAR BROTHERS, EVEN when I first came to you I didn't use lofty words and brilliant ideas to tell you <u>God's message.</u> ² For I decided that I would speak only of Jesus Christ and his death on the cross. ³ I came to you in weakness—timid and trembling. ⁴ And my preaching was very plain, not with a lot of oratory and human wisdom, but the <u>Holy Spirit's power was in my words,</u> proving to those who heard them that the <u>message was from God.</u> ⁵ I did this because I wanted your faith to stand firmly upon God, not on man's great ideas.

⁶ Yet when I am among mature Christians I do speak with words of great wisdom, but <u>not the kind that comes from here on earth,</u> and not the kind that appeals to the great men of this world,

who are doomed to fall. [7] Our words are wise because they are from God, telling of God's wise plan to bring us into the glories of heaven. This plan was hidden in former times, though it was made for our benefit before the world began. [8] But the great men of the world have not understood it; if they had, they never would have crucified the Lord of Glory.

[9] That is what is meant by the Scriptures which say that no mere man has ever seen, heard or even imagined what wonderful things God has ready for those who love the Lord. [10] But we know about these things because God has sent his Spirit to tell us, and his Spirit searches out and shows us all of God's deepest secrets. [11] No one can really know what anyone else is thinking, or what he is really like, except that person himself. And no one can know God's thoughts except God's own Spirit. [12] And God has actually given us his Spirit (not the world's spirit) to tell us about the wonderful free gifts of grace and blessing that God has given us. [13] In telling you about these gifts we have even used the very words given to us by the Holy Spirit, not words that we as men might choose. So we use the Holy Spirit's words to explain the Holy Spirit's facts.[a] [14] But the man who isn't a Christian can't understand and can't accept these thoughts from God, which the Holy Spirit teaches us. They sound foolish to him, because only those who have the Holy Spirit within them can understand what the Holy Spirits means. Others just can't take it in. [15] But the spiritual man has insight into

everything, and that bothers and baffles the man of the world, who can't understand him at all. [16] How could he? For certainly he has never been one to know the Lord's thoughts, or to discuss them with him, or to move the hands of God by prayer.[b] But, strange as it seems, we Christians actually do have within us a portion of the very thoughts and mind of Christ.

When Frances and I ask for a message from God, we "unzip" our mind like opening our head with a zipper. We don't try to think, but are receptive to the thoughts or messages from God. Yes, to the mind not controlled by the Holy Spirit, this seems foolish, but it works! I would like to be so "in the Spirit" at all times that I could always get an immediate answer from him. But then, I might want to make him my slave. He knows how to work best with us.

God has spoken to me audibly once, in silent words several times, in thoughts most of the time, by flooding me with peace, by bathing me in a bath of love, by revealing spiritual meanings in the Bible, by simply putting an answer into my mind without my awareness, and many other ways. But predominantly he speaks when my heart (my spirit) is seeking ways I can serve him. Some of these have been for my comfort or to please me. He wants to do that, too, you know.

I would like to share a few ways I have 'heard' God's instructions. Perhaps you have many other ways you have received answers. The Holy Spirit is wanting us to listen, and when we sincerely ask, he will answer. We can never operate in the supernatural realm as long as we stay in the realm where we can seemingly do it without God. I am adventuresome.

Before we were given a miracle ministry, we prayed for the healing of diseases, injuries and sickness. God would heal a person every once in awhile, then more frequently. We talked with each other about what was happening—and why and how. What was changing? We were aware that the power to heal came as a result of the Baptism of the Holy Spirit. By studying the way Jesus, Peter, James and John prayed, we began to see what we were doing that was similar to what they were doing. If a person had a stiff neck, we used to pray and "hope" they got healed. As our faith increased we would ask Jesus to touch the neck. Then in faith believing it was healed we would say, "Now bend your neck, move it! Turn it from side to side!" We discovered that when they acted, God acted, and miracles occurred much more frequently. How did we hear God speak: by research, thought, observation, experimenting, searching— our normal way of seeking an answer to what God wanted us to do.

This morning I had a dream just before I woke up (I know it was at that time because it woke me up). I have no idea whether this was a dream God put into my mind or not. I believe God can do this because he did it to Jacob—remember his ladder? God said ". . . old men shall dream dreams." (Acts 2:17) I am very careful about placing confidence

141

in a dream because it's easy to get hung up. Most dreams probably come from eating too much too late, or some such thing, instead of from God. In my life I generally ignore them other than to tell Frances about them if they are interesting.

This morning I was awakened by a dream—and with a bad attitude. Here is the dream—and my reaction. We were in a huge auditorium packed with people, the preliminaries of the service we were to conduct were already underway and it was about two minutes before we were to be on stage. We always like to be alone together, praying and praising God, giving him our minds so we can hear him tell us what we are to say and do. Not so this time! We got separated and I was rushing to try to get with her; I discovered I didn't have my coat and tie on. They had been wadded up and pitched on a dusty table—half way across the building. I was searching everywhere at once and when I finally got to where Frances was, she was as busy and frustrated as I. She was sitting at a little desk, thumbing rapidly through the yellow pages of a telephone directory, talking to two other people at the same time. Some lady was sitting next to her and I couldn't get close to her. Then—out of Frances' mouth came a curse word (in my dream). I was shocked, hurt, broken hearted and sick and said, "Frances, do you realize what you said!" Now, no swear word has ever come out of her mouth nor entered her mind since Jesus cleaned her mind of these habits right after she met him. I'm quite sure had this been a reality instead of a dream she would never have even thought this word. But it was very real to me this morning.

In my dream I lectured her very firmly—the very idea of having her mind on something like this at any time, especially just before we were to share the love of God with two or three thousand people—how could she do this. I said you had better stay back stage awhile and ask God's forgiveness while I start the service; and I suppose I said more than that! Then, in my dream I found my thoughts changing directions. I am the one responsible to protect her from all harm, and as it says in Eph. 5:25-26, I am to show her the same kind of love as Christ showed his bride, the church, when he died for her—*to make her holy and clean,* washed by baptism and God's Word. In my dream-thoughts I reasoned that *I* should have arranged a time for prayer; I should have been with her and should be showing her love instead of thinking every hurting expression I could find to point my finger at her. Suddenly I discovered *I* was stirring up all kinds of imaginary bad attitudes and was far deeper into the sin of bad attitudes than her dream sin of bad language.

Then I began setting aside my bad attitudes— pushing them away and thinking—I shouldn't criticize her (remind her, yes, but not dwell on it, belittling her). Had I not awakened, I would probably have been using worse words than she used. That's when I woke up!

Would you like to know what happened in my first moments awake, It took a second to prime my brain into functioning under my control. Jesus was my first thought, followed immediately by telling him I was sorry for my dream attitudes; then I looked at my Frances, sleeping beautifully at my side, as innocent as a little baby! I began thanking God for her, for her constant tender love for him, for me, and for the people she serves. Within a few seconds, my whole disturbed, frustrated, ulcerated attitude was redirected into a calmness and cleanliness that was enveloped wholly in the love of God. And Jesus said to the stormy waves "peace, be still" and the stormy waves of my emotions changed to calm waves of devotion! What a difference!

This was a true story that just happened this morning, but let me share the reason I'm writing it in this particular chapter. It's not important whether or not it was a dream from God or just one of the normal processes of a sleepy mind. It *is* important how God can talk to us when we are receptive not only to hearing his voice, but to wanting to be in our mind-attitude as he wants us to be. He said "For God is at work *within you,* helping you want to obey him, and then helping you do what he wants." (Phil. 2:13)

I could have awakened, said good morning to Jesus, cocked my ear toward heaven and waited for God to speak. I would never have heard him, because, you see, he is in me, helping me *want to obey him.* I *wanted* our ministry and our lives to be what he wanted. How did I discover what he wanted? God spoke to me! Really, you might say, I didn't read about that in what you just said. The Spirit of God in me had reminded me of my wrong attitude. I didn't just think of this. Because I want to be like he wants me, I am sensitive to his reminding silent, loving, drawing "voice." He blinded and deafened the Jews because they hardened their hearts and hated his laws. They didn't want to please God—they wanted to please themselves.

God gave "manna"—they wanted meat!

God gave "Jesus"—they wanted self!

I have searched with a hungry mind in my thoughts, in my attitudes, in my Bible—searching, storing away in my heart and mind, for ways I can please Jesus. I search for ways to please Frances and constantly find new ways to express my love, ways I can make her life easier, her day brighter— because I want to. I love her with all my human husband heart. I learn to love God and Jesus the same way. I do love them. I discover little new hidden treasures of principles Jesus taught. There is, for example, a rich vein of gold in the one principle "Trust me and obey me." You can never deplete that gold mine. "For if you give, you will get" (Luke 6:38). We give to God—then he gives to us. I give to Frances, and I get more love back than I give. By these and other little "spoken and written" words of God and Jesus, I have *"heard"* them say—test me, try me, prove me! Yes, I heard that voice when I searched the scriptures. Because my ears were receptive to that, other gold nuggets in the river bed of life washed to the surface and I "heard" more. Hearing can come when we want to hear. We can only want to hear when we want to obey. That's why it was important that I give *all* of my CPA practice to Jesus. I want to operate it like he wants me to. As I learned to do this, I discovered I could hear his advice, his instructions, his thoughts of wisdom and judgment—I want to do it HIS WAY!

By meditating on his specifications of how to operate our lives while in the Kingdom of Heaven—on earth, we learn how God, by his Spirit, communicates with us. It is easy, it is practical, it is certain, it is successful.

God uses the most simple, everyday, down-to-earth, unexpected ways to open our spirit-ears. Sometimes we might think it would be better if God occasionally missed hearing our thoughts. I'm glad he doesn't—I need his discipline. Look at this one:

We have a large rubber stamp which says:

GOD IS FABULOUS

On letters, bills, tax return envelopes and packages we mail from home, we boldly stamp these beautiful words.

I had overpaid a department store about $65.00 and had no purchase for several months, so I just left the credit balance. Finally, I made a purchase on credit. The bill came while we were on an extended tour and someway I didn't pay it until it was 31 days old. The next month I received a bill for I believe three cents. This irritated me because I don't like the 18% service charge and interest, and I always pay well on time. I politely wrote a note on the bill, explaining about my credit balance and that I had paid it just one day late. I asked that they please cancel the charge. The next month I received the bill with a three cent balance. This really irritated me—in fact I was angry about it. I curtly wrote them, explaining the circumstances as before, adding that I had been a good, on time paying customer for years and that if they didn't cancel the charge I would never be in the store again! They should have been glad I was a "totally dedicated Christian" or I would probably have used some words very unpleasing to them. I stuck it in the envelope, sealed it, put a stamp on and by habit I took our special stamp, hit the ink pad and raised my arm to stamp the envelope! Then, in that lightning fast way God does it, into my mind came: "What will happen if you have the opportunity to witness to the clerk who reads your note about how Jesus gives peace, love and patience! What is that clerk going to think about your attitude? I put the rubber stamp on the desk, opened the letter, removed my memorandum, inserted a check for three cents, put it back in the envelope, carefully placed the rubber stamp on the envelope saying. . . .

GOD IS FABULOUS

God spoke very plainly —
I listened intently —
I *wanted* to be like he wanted me to be —

"I continually discipline and punish everyone I love; so I must punish you, unless you turn from your indifference and become enthusiastic about the things of God." Rev. 3:19. Notice his "two way" communication system?

Hearing God is by faith. That doesn't mean we have to assume or imagine we hear him. We know we hear "HIM" when we have faith to believe he is talking. God's mighty Holy Spirit is given to all who ask and who have been born again spiritually. Faith is a gift which God wants to give.

We have the choice and ability to accept or reject thoughts—our own, God's, or the evil thoughts of Satan. Many people ask us to pray that they will not have "nasty" thoughts. God is quick to remind each of us of the fact that the thoughts are nasty, even as they approach our mental recognition. We can slam shut the door to our mind and lock it to block the entrance of an evil thought trying to get in to rob us of our relationship to God. We can also hear the approaching footsteps of a thought sent from God to bless us and slam shut that door to bar entrance, or throw it wide open and say welcome—come in! We have the choice. One of the most common examples of this is also the greatest of all opportunities—we can open or shut the door: The Holy Spirit convicts us by saying, "you are a sinner," and by saying, "you need to repent of your sins"; by promising, "you will be forgiven of all sins if you desire and are willing to do your part." Jesus says in Rev. 3:20, "Look! I have been standing at the door and I am constantly knocking. If anyone *hears me calling him* and opens the door, I will come in and fellowship with him and he with me." It would be very unusual for us to audibly hear Jesus say that, but I suppose every Christian has "heard" Jesus say it as the Holy Spirit puts it into our minds.

I would challenge anyone who really wants to go all the way into the depth of the Spirit World of God to "search their hearts and see if there be any wicked ways in them." Give their all to God, but stay in the same business they are in, unless God clearly removes them. Make sure they are born again in Christ Jesus, accept the baptism of the Holy Spirit, spend hundred of hours in the written Word of God, yielding their ways and attitudes, searching for new depth to do what Jesus and God want. Turn loose of Self!

then
FOLLOW JESUS
all the Way!

It's my understanding that everything which

enters your mind remains there during your lifetime, whether it enters by sight, hearing, touch, taste or smell. It then becomes a matter of recalling these memory sensations stored there. That makes it very important what we allow to be put into our minds.

Have you ever seen a lightning bug or firefly? They are seen just for an instant and then the light is gone and the image fades away. Try turning an electric light switch on and off quickly in the dark, looking directly at the light bulb. Notice how the image of the bulb remains in your mind's eye for an instant as it fades away. Try this simple experiment with me: Have someone select a picture, preferably one with which you are not familiar. If it's on a wall, close your eyes and turn toward it. If it's in a book, hold your place so you can quickly open the book to view it. Now— quickly look at the picture just for one second and then look away from it. Now recall: What was the picture? A mountain stream, a mountain, a house, a car? You saw the whole picture. Now name the details you saw in the picture. Were there flowers? Was it a moonlight scene? Was there a road? Were any people pictured? See how many details you can recall. Did you notice how the total image with all the details were impressed on your mind, all in a flash of a second.

When God "thinks" into our minds, he usually puts the entire thought, scriptures, events, solutions, stories or whatever he is saying, into our minds in a flash of a second. We can "grab" those thoughts and develop them by simply thinking the details through by our recall ability. When God reveals a thought, stop immediately and think through all he has said. Tell it to someone in detail if you can. This stores it into your human mind for remembrance.

Frances and I speak almost entirely without notes. As we are presenting a message, we have prayed and thought about it in a general way before. But while we are talking, we follow the thoughts which come into our minds. We have prayed, believing, that God would put the thoughts into our minds by his Spirit or block them from our minds, as he chooses. These thoughts come almost entirely from experiences we have had, miracles we have seen or read about, principles we have learned about in the Bible or otherwise—messages stored into our minds from times passed, but nevertheless, stored in our human brain. When the Holy Spirit, who knows the needs of the listeners, wants to tell them something through our voices, he recalls the right combination of stories, scriptures, or principles into our minds, and we speak them. We are awed by the accuracy of his speaking to receptive listeners just what they need to know. He flashes messages into our mind in a piece of a second that may take five or ten minutes to tell. For example, as I write this book, most of these words and thoughts have been spoken one time or many times before. The scriptures have been read and meditated upon many times. I prayed, Frances laid her hands on my head and prayed and several friends are praying as I write this chapter. Into my mind the book is being recalled as fast as I can write, and the stories and supporting details are falling into place like a computer card sorter or a collator of pages of a book.

I learned part of this principle of hearing God's silent voice, these Holy Spirit thoughts, from Luke 12:11-12: "And when you are brought to trial before these Jewish rulers and authorities in the synagogues, don't be concerned about what to say in your defense, for the Holy Spirit will give you the right words even as you are standing there." I not only read this, I tried it on several occasions and it worked. I also learned by trying it, to ask for answers before I stood before an audience. There were times before I listened in advance of speaking when I would start a second story as it came into my mind—before I gave the point of the first story, and that's not good. I'm still not immune to that, but I'm learning not only to open my mind for my next thoughts, but to keep it open for the thought in process at the time.

How to Make a Decision

Early one Sunday morning I was reading the Bible for two meditating hours. Suddenly I saw a scripture, then a flash of thoughts and another scripture that has helped in my business decisions many times since. I pray it will help you to hear God's thoughts for your business decisions.

I had been reading the book of I Samuel where the children of Israel were grumbling to God (that's not the best way to talk to him) because all the other nations had a king and they didn't, but wanted one. They went to Samuel and said" 'Give us a king like all the other nations have,' they pleaded. Samuel was terribly upset and went to the Lord for *advice.* 'Do as they say,' the Lord replied. for I am the one they are rejecting, not you—they don't want me to be their king any longer." (I Sam. 8:5-7) God granted their wish for a ruler physically, but never relinquished his kingship spiritually.

In the Old Testament days, God spoke and conducted his business largely through prophets or seers. Samuel was God's man at this time. God chose Saul to be the king. Saul was the most handsome man in Israel, and was head and shoulders taller than anyone else in the land! He was from the tribe of Benjamin, the smallest in Israel, and his family was the least important of all the families of the tribe. He was, and felt, unqualified to be king. But God chose him and gave full instructions in prophecy to Samuel.

Picture now this good looking giant, just having been treated like a king at his coronation banquet and look what Samuel did to him. "Then Samuel took a flask of oil and poured it over Saul's head and kissed him on the cheek and said, 'I am doing this because the Lord has appointed you to be the king of his people, Israel.' " (I Sam. 10:1) Before I learned that the Holy Spirit reveals spiritual truths, I read this and thought what a mess—oil poured all over his clothes just as he was ready to walk a long way back home. But then God, through his Spirit

153

language way of talking to Christians, made it simple to understand what happened. "Oil" throughout the Bible is symbolic of the Holy Spirit. God was their Spiritual king and was to lead his people by his Holy Spirit through a mere man, Saul. So, what happened was that the Holy Spirit was poured over his head—he had the anointing of God so God would remain king through him.

Now, skip over to the 6th and 7th verses and see how God would rule his people through him. "At that time the Spirit of the Lord will come mightily upon you, and you will prophesy with them and you will feel and act like a different person. From that time on your decisions should be based on whatever seems best under the circumstances, *for the Lord will guide you.*"

In my accounting practice I have learned tax laws and financial matters adequately to serve my clients as their CPA. Always I have made decisions for them based upon my knowledge applied with my judgment under the circumstances. But God floodlighted something else about how my decisions should be made. He said, "your decisions should be based on whatever seems best under the circumstances, *FOR THE LORD WILL GUIDE YOU.* I nearly jumped out of my chair when I saw this. I have received the same Holy Spirit Saul had. I am an ordinary man like Saul was. He was operating a business like I was. What's the difference? He accepted his heritage—I hadn't recognized *God's voice*, his Word, before that morning. I had actually done my work normally and received answers in my business problems, but this

154

was God saying, "Charles, your decisions should be based on whatever seems best under the circumstances, and *I will guide you by my Spirit.* I knew from the eighth chapter of Romans that those who follow after the Holy Spirit find themselves doing those things that please God. And that following after the Holy Spirit leads to life and peace.

One of my very favorite chapters in the Bible is the first chapter of James. Look what it says about decisions. I will underscore to direct your attention as the Holy Spirit directed mine.

1 FROM: JAMES, A servant of God and of the Lord Jesus Christ.

To: Jewish Christians scattered everywhere. Greetings!

2 Dear brothers, is your life full of difficulties and temptations? Then be happy, 3 for when the way is rough, your patience has a chance to grow. 4 So let it grow, and don't try to squirm out of your problems. For when your patience is finally in full bloom, then you will be ready for anything, strong in character, full and complete.

5 If you want to know what God wants you to do, ask him, and he will gladly tell you, for he is always ready to give a bountiful supply of wisdom to all who ask him; he will not resent it. 6 But when you ask him, be sure that you really expect him to tell you, for a doubtful mind will be as unsettled as a wave of the sea that is driven and tossed by the wind; 7,8 and every decision you then make will be uncertain, as you turn first this way,

Notice, the provision doesn't say, "ask God for any answer *you want.*" It says, "if you want to know what *God wants* you to do." If your business belongs to God, you can ask him anything about it. That means a lot to me in connection with the "if it be thy will" scripture prayer. If it's God's business decision, it is God's will. Maybe the examination should be of ourselves and our motives and searchingly pray—*am* I your will? If I am God's will, I'm in God's will, so I can ask him anything I want to know and get my answer. Trusting God now comes into the art of conversation with God. If you don't trust him to answer—if you don't ask with faith, don't expect the Lord to give you any solid answers—every *decision* you then make will be uncertain, as you turn first this way, and then that.

When we drive a car our minds don't have to meditate on how to make it change directions, how to make it stop, how to make it go faster or slower. This has become so much a part of our mind that it is done seemingly without thinking. But, praise God, our mind is thinking—or we would quickly wreck the car. We trust our minds and the car to do all we want them to do; and we can sing, think or talk while our mind and the car are doing these routine, habit jobs. We don't need to ask God how to shift gears or turn the steering wheel, but we can ask him to guide our decisions and to protect us as we travel. If we are sincerely working as wisely as we know how, I believe he will guide us so our decisions, made with our own minds, will match his decisions, just like he told King Saul. Look at a couple more "decision" verses:

I Samuel 16:7

7 But the Lord said to Samuel, "Don't judge by a man's face or height, for this is not the one. I don't make decisions the way you do! Men judge by outward appearance, but I look at a man's thoughts and intentions."

Romans 11:33-36

33 Oh, what a wonderful God we have! How great are his wisdom and knowledge and riches! How impossible it is for us to understand his decisions and his methods! 34 For who among us can know the mind of the Lord? Who knows enough to be his counselor and guide? 35 And who could ever offer to the Lord enough to induce him to act? 36 For everything comes from God alone. Everything lives by his power, and everything is for his glory. To him be glory evermore.

I have a millionaire client whom I respect highly for his success, his wisdom, and his judgment. He respects my guidance, loyalty and judgment as his CPA. To me CPA means, wherever I am, "Christ's Personal Ambassador." (See II Cor. 5:20.) We have worked together for years successfully and in harmony. He knows that he should never do anything of significance without first reviewing the income tax consequences with me. There's only been one problem—he waits until the last minute to tell me and I seem never to have adequate time to research difficult tax matters.

One morning a call came to me from him. He said he was going into a business venture on a $2,000,000.00 project with another man, and could he come by at 4:30 that afternoon to review it with me. The appointment was made and promptly at 4:30 he came in with his project partner. His partner is a Jew lawyer. If you are ever involved with a Jew lawyer, be sure he is on your side, because he's probably very smart, swift talking, shrewd, and out to win his case. Such was this Jew lawyer. As soon as we sat down, he said he was going to talk fast because he didn't like to pay accounting fees, and besides, his tax lawyers and accountants had already worked out the tax plan for the venture, so all he wanted was my approval for my client. I never heard anyone talk so fast in my life, so I stopped him about the second minute (about 10,000 words later) and said wait a minute. I want to know every detail about this venture, so please talk slowly and explain carefully. He agreed and began explaining one of the most complex tax structures in which I was ever involved. He said they were to sign the papers the first thing the next morning. I realized I had no time to do tax research or extensive thinking, so while he was explaining I was intently listening, but I was rushing a plea to heaven. I flashed a

158

thought, intact (without putting it into words)—
help!

One thing this Jew lawyer didn't know—*I HAD
A JEW LAWYER, TOO!* I was really in consulta-
tion with him!!! Praise Jesus!! I had told Jesus I
didn't have time for research, and asked him to
give me the answer quickly. When the lawyer
finished explaining, I began talking. For about ten
minutes one of the most beautiful tax plans to a
very complicated situation came pouring out of
my mouth as though I was reading from a printed
document. And I really was just about doing that
as the Holy Spirit supernaturally brought tax laws
and practical experiences of twenty years rushing
from all directions into my recall mechanism as
though drawn by a magnet, and then sorted the
input like a computer selector to give me the
answer!

When I quit talking, the lawyer just stared at
me and said, "Why didn't my tax men think of
that?" "When you are guided by the Holy Spirit
you need no longer obey *Jewish* laws!!" (Galatians
5:18)

This is not always the way God has solved my
tax problems, but he did a special miracle that
day. He most often has me *do what seems best
under the circumstances*—research in our tax
library for the answer. When he does this, I ask
him to alert my mind and guide me to the answer,
and then to see that I recognize the answer and
apply it correctly—*for the Lord will guide me.*

Our part of the world into which we are to go

and preach the Good News includes our business associates. People who have not been born again and are not following after the Holy Spirit, cannot understand what we are talking about spiritually, "But the man who isn't a Christian can't understand and can't accept these *thoughts* from God, which the Holy Spirit teaches us. They sound foolish to him, because only those who have the Holy Spirit within them can understand what the Holy Spirit means. Others just can't take it in." (I Cor. 2:14) Then how can we in business convince our associates that Jesus is the answer to life?

They know we are Christians—you just don't keep that fact covered up with a basket of shame if you are really in love with Jesus. Most of them know when you are acting like they think a Christian should and when you are not. They look at you as a business man or woman, not as a Christian, and watch your business and personal conduct. What should our conduct be? Let's look at a few of God's standards for the business man or woman:

Romans 12:9-11

WORK WITH

A WOW!!

⁹ Don't just pretend that you love others: really love them. Hate what is wrong. Stand on the side of the good. ¹⁰ Love each other with brotherly affection and take delight in honoring each other. ¹¹ Never be lazy in your work but serve the Lord enthusiastically.

A friend who had recently received the baptism of the Holy Spirit and became a fireball for Jesus was having trouble getting his work done—he couldn't stop talking about Jesus. He asked me if I thought he ought to continue doing a good job for his customers, or what? I said no longer should he try to do a good job—he should be satisfied with no less than a *superior* job. And also learn to do the superior job first and then talk about Jesus. I learned this from personal experience of overwitnessing.

Ephesians 6:5-9: Substitute employer and employee instead of master and slave:

WATCH
ME,
JESUS

[5] Slaves, obey your masters; be eager to give them your very best. Serve them as you would Christ. [6,7] Don't work hard only when your master is watching and then shirk when he isn't looking; work hard and with gladness all the time, as though working for Christ, doing the will of God with all your hearts. [8] Remember, the Lord will pay you for each good thing you do, whether you are slave or free.

And you slave owners must treat your slaves right, just as I have told them to treat you. Don't keep threatening them; remember, you yourselves are slaves to Christ; you have the same Master they do, and he has no favorites.

Philippians 2:14

BE

MY

FLASHLIGHT

[14] In everything you do, stay away from complaining and arguing, [15] so that no one can speak a word of blame against you. You are to live clean, innocent lives as children of God in a dark world full of people who are crooked and stubborn. Shine out among them like beacon lights, [16] holding out to them the Word of Life.

Philippians 4:8-9

CAUTION -

MIND

CONSTRUCTION

[8] And now, brothers, as I close this letter let me say this one more thing: Fix your thoughts on what is true and good and right. Think about things that are pure and lovely, and dwell on the fine, good things in others. Think about all you can praise God for and be glad about. [9] Keep putting into practice all you learned from me and saw me doing, and the God of peace will be with you.

Philippians 4:11-13

For I have learned how to get along happily whether I have much or

162

ULCERS

REMOVED

FREE

Colossians 3:22-25

SMILE, YOU

ARE ON DISPLAY

FOR JESUS!

little. [12] I know how to live on almost nothing or with everything. I have learned the secret of contentment in every situation, whether it be a full stomach or hunger, plenty or want; [13] for I can do everything God asks me to with the help of Christ who gives me the strength and power.

[22] You slaves must always obey your earthly masters, not only trying to please them when they are watching you but all the time; obey them willingly because of your love for the Lord and because you want to please him.

Work *hard* and *cheerfully* at all you do, just as though you were working for the Lord and not merely for your masters, remembering that *it is the Lord Christ who is going to pay you* giving you your full portion of all he owns. *He is the one you are really working for.* And if you don't do *your very best* for him, he will pay you in a way that you won't like—for he has no special favorites who can get away with *shirking.*

II Thess. 3:6-10

[6] Now here is a command, dear brothers, given

NO
LOAFING
ALLOWED

in the name of our Lord Jesus Christ by his authority: Stay away from any Christian who spends his days in laziness and does not follow the ideal of hard work we set up for you. [7] For you well know that you ought to follow our example: you never saw us loafing; [8] we never accepted food from anyone without buying it; we worked hard day and night for the money we needed to live on, in order that we would not be a burden to any of you. [9] It wasn't that we didn't have the right to ask you to feed us, but we wanted to show you, firsthand, how you should work for your living. [10] Even while we were still there with you we gave you this rule: "He who does not work shall not eat."

[11] Yet we hear that some of you are living in laziness, refusing to work, and wasting your time in gossiping. [12] In the name of the Lord Jesus Christ we appeal to such people—we command them—to quiet down, get to work, and earn their own living. [13] And to the rest of

you I say, dear brothers, never be tired of doing right.

I Tim. 6:1-2

BE THE BEST EMPLOYEE OR EMPLOYER

I Tim. 6:6-10

MAKE A FORTUNE

6 CHRISTIAN SLAVES SHOULD work hard for their owners and respect them; never let it be said that Christ's people are poor workers. Don't let the name of God or his teaching be laughed at because of this. [2] If their owner is a Christian, that is no excuse for slowing down; rather they should work all the harder because a brother in the faith is being helped by their efforts.

[6] Do you want to be truly rich? You already are if you are happy and good. [7] After all, we didn't bring any money with us when we came into the world, and we can't carry away a single penny when we die. [8] So we should be well satisfied without money if we have enough food and clothing. [9] But people who long to be rich soon begin to do all kinds of wrong things to get money, things that hurt them and

make them evil-minded and finally send them to hell itself. ¹⁰ For the love of money is the first step toward all kinds of sin. Some people have even turned away from God because of their love for it, and as a result have pierced themselves with many sorrows.

I Tim. 6:17-19

SAFE
INVESTMENTS!
HERE

¹⁷ Tell those who are rich not to be proud and not to trust in their money, which will soon be gone, but their pride and trust should be in the living God who always richly gives us all we need for our enjoyment. ¹⁸ Tell them to use their money to do good. They should be rich in good works and should give happily to those in need, always being ready to share with others whatever God has given them. ¹⁹ By doing this they will be storing up real treasure for themselves in heaven— it is the only safe investment for eternity! And they will be living a fruitful Christian life down here as well.

EXPECT GOD TO ACT! (Psalms 42:11)

God speaks by action—physical replies to our requests. It had been about three years in May of 1974 that we had known Frances had an enlarged heart. It wasn't particularly bothering her, we didn't think. But during the year preceding May, something seemed to be happening. Her energy would simply leave and she would be so tired all over that she could not force herself to go into a day's work. With Christ's mighty energy at work within her, she almost always could accelerate her energies to conduct services in Jesus' name. So often when we were nome she would sleep for two days, not even wanting to get up for food sometimes not being able to. She would repeatedly say to me—"I'm so tired, I'm so tired!" She never missed a service because of this, and miracle services require long hours standing, pouring out not only physical energy, but spiritual energy as well.

Then seemingly not related to this, she periodically would have blasting, bursting headaches. We prayed,—over and over and over asking God, thanking him, praising him. She took aspirin soaked in prayer. But nothing would ever diminish the pain. These would last about 24-48 hours and then would subside. Twice, because of the pain which was so bad that she would get violently ill, vomiting, she couldn't go any further. Once in Chicago I left her in bed all day with excruciating pain as I fulfilled our commitment. Except for

God and for Jesus, nothing would have separated us at that time. The spells began to come more often, until finally in May she really had a violent attack.

It had continued for almost 24 hours. I was constantly in prayer, but seemingly my prayers went no further than my intellect. There was no faith available, and you cannot attain faith on your own—it is a gift. Gifts are given because of a willing desire of the giver, and I found long ago they are not obtained by begging. Maybe we will get the gift, but it really becomes charity (as in poverty), not as "love" charity. I had no faith, but prayed anyway. Of course, the foundation of faith is belief in God and Christ Jesus, not in results or feeling. Others were praying but the pains never let up.

Finally about four o'clock in the afternoon we called our Spirit-filled doctor. He had been her doctor for almost five years (mine for over twenty years). He was the one who told her three years earlier about the enlarged heart. He had checked her in his clinic often and knew her medical history. We called him and Frances said,

"Could this be high blood pressure?"

"Yes, you have all the symptoms."

He prescribed some blood-pressure medication and instructed her to take it and said there should be a significant change in two hours; if it had not subsided to call him and he would come to our home (we live about 25 miles from him). Two hours passed and it was just as bad as before. I never left her bedside and prayed constantly, helplessly.

A friend who had experience as a medical technician came to the house with a sphygmomanometer, the instrument used to measure blood pressure. She immediately made the pressure test, and even after the medication had been in Frances about 2½ hours, the pressure was 225/140, much too high for comfort, and we assumed it had been even higher. She said she could tell that the heart was greatly enlarged as she placed a stethoscope on her body. She said she could also hear a whistling sound which indicated a hole in the heart or near it, like escaping air.

And then it happened!

I have explained how God imprints into our minds a complete thought or series of thoughts all at once—like looking at a picture and having the entire picture imprinted into our mind through our eyes in a split second. Into my mind, like an imprinted picture, came at lightning speed several thoughts, in sequence but like a ricocheting bullet. It was all in my mind in perhaps 1/10 of a second. I know the voice of God and knew he had spoken and in about another 1/10 second I was on my feet, standing over Frances! The technician friend had the blood pressure tester in her lap, and had no idea what was happening to me. She knows prayer so my action didn't surprise her. This is what happened:

About three months before, a Spirit-filled young woman had told us a true story, and God flashed that story into my memory recall. She had moved into an apartment in the southern part of the nation. The first night she had occasion to go into the kitchen and when she turned on the light, she was shocked to see large cockroaches all over the place. She was scared, disgusted and frustrated all at the same time. In contemplating what to do, she said she remembered something in the Bible and instantly pointed at the cockroaches and said, "God, you gave Adam dominion over all creeping things, so you creeping cockroaches, I take authority over you in the name of Jesus, and if you don't get out of here right now, I'm going to stomp you to death." She said they ran in every direction, disappeared and she hasn't seen them since.

When the Holy Spirit flashed that into my mind, I knew instantly that I was to speak to the heart, with the authority of Jesus. I knew Jesus spoke to fever in Peter's mother-in-law and said "fever, I rebuke you" and she was healed. Then I thought, "Is it a spirit causing this?" If it was, I knew by Matthew 12 that I would bind Satan by the power of the Holy Spirit, and then with the authority of Jesus, command the spirit to come out, in Jesus' name. But like a bouncing echo, the story of Jesus calming the stormy sea came flashing into my mind. He didn't cast out a spirit of storm. He just spoke with authority to the wind and waves and said, "Peace, be still!" and the sea became calm.

Then in a mini-second came the recall of Mark 16:14-20:

> [14] Still later he appeared to the eleven disciples as they were eating together. He rebuked them for their unbelief—their

stubborn refusal to believe those who had seen him alive from the dead.

[15] And then he told them, "You are to go into all the world and preach the Good News to everyone, everywhere. [16] Those who believe and are baptized will be saved. But those who refuse to believe will be condemned.

[17] "And those who believe shall use my authority to cast out demons, and they shall speak new languages.[c] [18] They will be able even to handle snakes with safety, and if they drink anything poisonous, it won't hurt them; and they will be able to place their hands on the sick and heal them."

[19] When the Lord Jesus had finished talking with them, he was taken up into heaven and sat down at God's right hand.

[20] And the disciples went everywhere preaching, and the Lord was with them and confirmed what they said by the miracles that followed their messages.

I knew from these scriptures that the authority for miracles came from Jesus. Immediately, armed with the series of thoughts, I pointed at Frances' heart and spoke out loud. With the authority of a policeman ordering a criminal to move, I said: "Heart, I take authority over you, in the name of Jesus, I command you blood-pressure, go down to normal! In the name of Jesus, blood-pressure, go down! By the authority of Jesus, and that means 'all' the authority of Jesus, not just a small pinch, but ALL the authority of Jesus, I command you in Jesus' name drop to normal!" "Heart, I command you, be healed and return to normal size. Jesus, heal the hole in the heart!"

I noticed another test was being made with the blood-testing instrument, and the lady was writing the results on a pad. I never stopped talking to the heart. Faith was there strong from God and there was no holding me back or questioning the Spirit. I had many times spoken to fever in babies, or grown people, in Jesus' name, commanding it to leave, and it had instantly left. I had felt burning, fever ridden heads cool immediately under my hand as Jesus touched the person. I had seen pain leave instantly after being constantly in a woman's leg for ten years as a result of a car wreck injury. Jesus had many times demonstrated that he had given us his authority and that it was the power of God's Spirit that healed. I was not playing games! I was not saying words! I was speaking to an enemy attacking my beloved Frances and hurting her severely, and I didn't like that enemy!

I continued talking to the heart and commanding the pressure to go down to normal for twelve minutes! I could see the lady getting excited as every minute or two she would test the pressure and write it down! I wasn't watching her, but could see her in my peripheral vision—my mind was on the business at hand! I did perceive an excitement in her and thought her wig might fly off any minute!

At the end of twelve minutes, she said, "It's normal!" Frances said the headache was gone! How we shouted praises to God!!!

We called our doctor and told him what had happened. We made an appointment for Frances to be admitted to the hospital for extensive tests. We believe in divine miracles, and have seen God do thousands of remarkable healings in front of our eyes as we watch his mighty Power at work! We also believe, as Jesus did when he put Dr. Luke on his staff, that doctors are in the medical department of the kingdom of God on earth.

The tests were made—X-rays, EKG's, calm tests, exertion tests, and I guess every test that is known to medical science. The results: no enlarged heart! No hole in the heart or evidence of it! Blood pressure normal! Blood pressure normal under exertion. CASE DISMISSED!!! Hallelujah!!!

Frances has had beautiful strength and health ever since that glorious night in May when Jesus, the Great Physician, stood over the bed, living in me, just a mere human being, and healed her sick body. She has had no more headaches, and her blood pressure is normal. All praise and honor and glory goes to God, our blessed heavenly Father, through his magnificent Son, Jesus!

All hail the power of Jesus' name!
Let angels prostrate fall,
Bring forth the royal diadem,
And crown him Lord of ALL!

Can we hear God speak? YES, we can. Does he want to instruct us daily in our normal events of the day? Yes, he does. We were created to have fellowship (communion, communication) with our God, our creator! Within my heart I feel I am just

173

entering into a new world, a Spirit world of God's glory and companionship, just as real as the one Adam experienced before his spirit world was taken away because of sin. The more I step beyond the realm of human capabilities, trusting God and Jesus—simply believing, the more excited I get of the great dimension in which we can live—and still successfully live and operate within our business world. I believe anyone who is willing can attain this level of communication with God—and even more!

I intend to search for, live for, experiment to attain a greater measure of the phenomenal power I believe God wants us to use for his glory. I intend to test him, try him and let him prove his promise that he will open the windows of heaven even more in communicating his desires to us!

AND JESUS SAID "FOLLOW ME"

Where do we go when we follow Jesus?
  Where he leads me, I will follow!
How do we find where he is so we will know
  Where to go to find him?
Do we find his footprints in the snow
  And follow them until we catch him?
What is he doing while we are following him?
  Is it interesting to be with him constantly?
Is he fun to live with? Is he exciting? Does he ever
gripe or complain?
  Is it relaxing to be around him or are we
  inclined to be tense and find it difficult to talk
  to him?

I was ready and anxious to get started on another chapter of this book early one morning, but I was drawn by the Spirit to spend a little more time alone with Jesus in the Bible before writing. I had been reading in Matthew from the New International Version. By the time I had read thirty minutes, I knew God had shown me the footsteps of Jesus—just some of them, but enough to know what he meant when he said *FOLLOW ME!* There's a segment of Matthew from Chapter 3 to Chapter 10 where Jesus instructed his newly

chosen disciples. Let him instruct us as we
FOLLOW HIM:

3:8   "Produce fruit in keeping with repentance."
FOLLOW ME into repentance.

3:11   "He (Jesus) will baptize you with the
Holy Spirit."
FOLLOW ME—Into fire and power—
surrender all.

3:16-17   He (John) saw the Spirit of God de-
scending like a dove and a voice from
heaven said, "This is my beloved Son,
whom I love; with him I am well
pleased."
FOLLOW ME—I am worthy—I am
God's divine Son.

4:10   Jesus said to him, "Away from me,
Satan! For it is written:
"Worship the Lord your God, and serve
him only.' "
FOLLOW ME—as I follow my Father.

4:17   "From that time on Jesus began to
preach, 'Repent, for the Kingdom of
Heaven is near.' "
FOLLOW ME—into salvation—you
must be born again!

4:19   "Come, follow me," Jesus said, "and I
will make you fishers of men."
FOLLOW ME—make my Father rich by
adding to his kindgom!

4:23   Jesus went through Galilee *teaching* in their synagogues, *preaching* the good news of the kingdom, and *healing* every disease and sickness among the people.
FOLLOW ME—go into all the world—and signs and wonders will follow! teach, preach, heal!

5:14   "You are the light of the world."
FOLLOW ME—let the world see Jesus—shine!

5:19   "Anyone who breaks one of the least of these commandments and teaches others to do the same will be called least in the kingdom of heaven, but whoever practices and teaches these commandments will be called great in the kingdom of heaven."
FOLLOW ME—love God, Jesus, neighbor as much as self, Love, Love, Love!

5:44   "But I tell you, love your enemies."
FOLLOW ME—Love, Love, Love, Love!

5:48   "Be perfect, therefore, as your heavenly Father is perfect."
FOLLOW ME—trust me, obey me, want to please me!

6:2   "So when you give to the needy. . . ."
FOLLOW ME—I gave to them food, health, love, blessings, . . . myself.

6:14   "For if you forgive men when they sin against you, your heavenly Father will also forgive you."

FOLLOW ME—Father, forgive them,
for they know not what they do—
forgive without reason.

6:21   "For where your treasure is, there your
heart will be also."
FOLLOW ME—in the same way, any of
you who does not give up everything he
has, cannot be my disciple.

6:24   "No one can serve two masters."
FOLLOW ME—I am your Master—if
you want me to be!

6:25   "Therefore I tell you, do not worry
about your life, what you eat or drink;
or about your body, what you will
wear."
FOLLOW ME—do you believe me? I
will care for you—abundantly!

6:33   "But seek first his kingdom and his
righteousness, and all these things will
be given to you as well."
FOLLOW ME—I am your source.

7:1   "Do not judge, or you too will be
judged. For in the same way you judge
others, you will be judged, and with the
measure you use, it will be measured to
you."
FOLLOW ME—you be my disciple and
I'll be the judge—you love, I'll pay.

7:7   "Ask and it will be given you; seek and
you will find; knock and the door will

be opened to you. For everyone who asks receives; he who seeks finds; and to him who knocks, the door will be opened."

FOLLOW ME—yes, it's me; come on in—to heaven.

7:12   "In everything do to others what you would have them do to you, for this sums up the Law and the Prophets."

FOLLOW ME—whatever you think about or say to others—just say the same thing to me—with the same attitude.

7:14   "But small is the gate and narrow the road that leads to life, and only a few find it."

FOLLOW ME—I'll lead you into heaven—I am the way, the truth and the life.

7:16   "By their fruit you will recognize them."

FOLLOW ME—my fruit is love, joy, peace, patience, kindness, goodness, faithfulness, gentleness, and self-control—this is what I subsist on; when you are with me, eat freely.

7:21   "Only he who does the will of my Father who is in heaven will enter the kingdom of heaven."

FOLLOW ME—I have obeyed in all things, even in voluntary death.

7:24   "Therefore, everyone who hears these words of mine and puts them into practice is like a wise man who built his house on the rock."

FOLLOW ME—I am the Rock Foundation.

8:3   "I am willing—be clean!"

:7   "I will go and heal him."

:16   "He drove out the spirits with a word. . . ."

FOLLOW ME—greater things than I do, you will do, when you believe.

8:18   "Teacher, I will follow you wherever you go."

"Lord, first let me go and bury my father."

FOLLOW ME—now, if you mean it!

8:23   "Lord, save us! We're going to drown!"

FOLLOW ME— am your salvation.

9:4   "Why do you entertain evil thoughts in your hearts?"

FOLLOW ME—whatsoever things are pure . . . only the holy shall see God.

9:9   Jesus saw Matthew, a tax collector. "Follow Me" and "Matthew got up and followed him."

FOLLOW ME—without questioning where or why or how.

10:1   "He called his twelve disciples to him and gave them authority to drive out evil spirits and to cure every kind of disease.

FOLLOW ME—and you will receive power when the Holy Spirit comes on you; and you will be my witnesses—everywhere you go. . . .

In your church—talk about me.

On your job—talk about me

In school—talk about me.

Whoever acknowledges me before men, I will also acknowledge him before my Father in heaven.

10:37-39 "Anyone who loves his father or mother more than me is not worthy of me; anyone who loves his son or daughter more than me is not worthy of me. Whoever finds his life will lose it, and whoever loses his life for my sake will find it."

FOLLOW ME—yes, Jesus, with all my heart I will follow you—I give you my whole life.

Jesus is saying:

ARE *YOU* WILLING?

TO FOLLOW ME into repentance?

TO FOLLOW ME into fire and power?

TO FOLLOW ME because I am worthy?

TO FOLLOW ME as I follow my Father?

TO FOLLOW ME into salvation and be born again?

TO FOLLOW ME and make my Father rich
by adding to his kingdom?

TO FOLLOW ME and go into all the world?

TO FOLLOW ME and let the world see me?

TO FOLLOW me and love my Father, me,
and your neighbor as much as you love
yourself?

TO FOLLOW me and love?

TO FOLLOW ME and trust me, obey me
and want to please me?

TO FOLLOW ME and give of yourself?

TO FOLLOW ME and forgive them?

TO FOLLOW ME and give up everything to
be my disciple?

TO FOLLOW ME and no other master?

TO FOLLOW ME and trust me to be your
source?

TO FOLLOW ME and be my disciple?

TO FOLLOW ME through the narrow gate?

TO FOLLOW ME and have all the fruit of
the Spirit?

TO FOLLOW ME because I am the Rock
Foundation?

TO FOLLOW ME without questioning
where or why or how?

TO FOLLOW ME and receive all the power
you need?

To FOLLOW ME and love me more than the
rest of the world?

Can you see Jesus standing in front of you,
crooking his finger toward you, saying "Come,
follow me?" Can you feel his presence drawing

you into discipleship? Has he put into your heart a hunger to go all the way from self to him as Master of your life? Has he chosen you to be one of his disciples today—in the world where you live and work? Are you willing to accept the assignment of following him, no matter what the cost? Are you willing to give him ALL? NOW? FOREVER???

If you have decided to follow Jesus, pray with me!

Lord Jesus!

I see you standing before me, crooking your finger, calling me to follow you wherever you go for the rest of my life on earth. I want with all of my heart to do whatever you want me to do! Take all of my life and make me spiritually what you want me to be! I am turning loose all of me I have held back. Forgive me of all of my sins! I never want to be lukewarm again, so please, Jesus, baptize me with the Holy Spirit and fire! I ask you to give me the promised power, and I will be your witness with my life, my actions, my language, my attitudes, my searching for all of God in my life; in holy living, in the use of my time, my energies, my reading, into whatever world of people you take me. I want to and will follow you! Thank you for choosing me and accepting me as one of your disciples. I LOVE YOU, JESUS! I WORSHIP YOU, I ADORE YOU, I PRAISE YOU! You are my Savior, my Redeemer, the Perfect Lamb of God, my Master, my Baptizer. You are King of Kings and Lord of Lords!

Worthy is the Lamb, who was slain,
   to receive power and wealth and wisdom

and strength and honor and glory and
praise!
Thank you, Jesus!

Freely you have received, freely give!

FOLLOW ME
FOLLOW ME
FOLLOW ME
FOLLOW ME
FOLLOW ME
FOLLOW ME
FOLLOW ME
FOLLOW ME
FOLLOW ME
FOLLOW ME
FOLLOW ME
FOLLOW ME
FOLLOW ME
FOLLOW ME
FOLLOW ME
FOLLOW ME
FOLLOW ME
FOLLOW ME
FOLLOW ME